Édouard Glissant

Treatise on the Whole-World

THE GLISSANT TRANSLATION PROJECT

Édouard Glissant

Treatise on
the Whole-World

translated by
Celia Britton

LIVERPOOL UNIVERSITY PRESS

First published 2020 by
Liverpool University Press
4 Cambridge Street
Liverpool
L69 7ZU

Copyright © 2020 Liverpool University Press

The right of Celia Britton to be identified as the translator of this book has been asserted by her in accordance with the Copyright, Designs and Patents Act 1988.

All rights reserved. No part of this book may be reproduced, stored in a retrieval system, or transmitted, in any form or by any means, electronic, mechanical, photocopying, recording, or otherwise, without the prior written permission of the publisher.

British Library Cataloguing-in-Publication data
A British Library CIP record is available

ISBN 978-1-78962-098-6 cased
ISBN 978-1-78962-131-0 limp

Typeset by Carnegie Book Production, Lancaster

A Timeline for Édouard Glissant

21 September 1928	Édouard Godard is born in the Morne Bezaudin, Martinique.
1935–1939	Primary school, Le Lamentin, Martinique.
1938	Édouard Godard is recognized by his father and becomes Édouard Glissant.
1939–1945	High school.
1944	Glissant founds and directs a journal, *Franc Jeu*.
1946	He leaves Martinique to study ethnology and philosophy (under the philosopher Jean Wahl) in France, at the Université de la Sorbonne.
1948	Publication of Glissant's first poems in the journal *Les temps modernes*, founded by Jean-Paul Sartre and Simone de Beauvoir.
1950	Glissant marries Yvonne Suvélor in Paris. He collaborates with the journal *Présence africaine*.
1952	He receives a Master of Arts in Philosophy. His thesis, under Gaston Bachelard's direction, is entiled *Découverte et conception du monde dans la poésie contemporaine*.
1953	Glissant contributes to the journal *Les Lettres nouvelles*, founded by Maurice Nadeau and Maurice Saillet. *Un champ d'îles* (poems) (Paris, Instance).
1955	*La terre inquiète* (poems) (Paris, éditions du Dragon).
1956	*Les Indes* (poem) (Paris, Le Seuil). *Soleil de la conscience, Poétique I* (essays) (Paris, Le Seuil). Glissant participates in the first congress of black writers and artists in Paris.

1958	*La Lézarde* (novel) (Paris, Le Seuil), which receives the Théophraste Renaudot Prize.
1959	Glissant participates in the second congress of black writers and artists in Rome.
1960	*Le sel noir* (poems) (Paris, Le Seuil). Glissant participates in the FAGA (Front Antillo-Guyanais pour l'Autonomie). He signs the *Manifeste des 121* or *Declaration on the right of insubordination in the Algerian War*.
1961	*Le sang rivé* (poems) (Paris, Le Seuil). Visit to Cuba. Glissant is forbidden to stay in Martinique and assigned to reside in Metropolitan France, as one of the leaders of Antillean separatism.
1964	*Le Quatrième Siècle* (novel) (Paris, Le Seuil). Glissant marries Jacqueline Marie Amélie Hospice in Paris.
1965	Glissant is allowed to return to Martinique.
1967	He creates the *Institut Martiniquais d'Études* (IME), a private school, where many artists and writers will be taught.
1969	*L'Intention poétique, Poétique II* (essays) (Paris, Le Seuil).
1971	Glissant founds the journal *Acoma*, hosted by the Parisian publisher Maspéro.
1975	*Malemort* (novel), (Paris, Le Seuil).
1978	*Monsieur Toussaint* (theatre play) (Paris, Le Seuil).
1979	*Boises* (poems) (éditions Acoma, Martinique).
1980	He defends his PhD in sociology at the Sorbonne University with *summa cum laude*.
1981	*Le Discours antillais* (essay) (Paris, Le Seuil), based on his PhD. *La case du commandeur* (novel) (Paris, Le Seuil).
1982–1988	Director of the *Courrier de l'Unesco*. Glissant meets Sylvie Sémavoine.
1985	*Pays rêvé, pays réel* (poems) (Paris, Le Seuil).
1987	*Mahogany* (novel) (Paris, Le Seuil).
1988	Glissant is named distinguished professor and director of the Center for French and Francophone Studies at Louisiana State University.

1989	Doctor *honoris causa* from the Collège universitaire de Glendon, University of York, Canada. Wins the Puterbaugh Prize and lectures at the University of Oklahoma, Norman, under the aegis of *World Literature Today*.
1990	Glissant moves from Le Seuil to Gallimard. *Poétique de la Relation, Poétique III* (essay) (Paris, Gallimard). *Discours de Glendon* (essay) (Toronto, editions du GREF). Director of the Caribbean Carbet Prize.
1991	*Fastes* (poems) (Toronto, éditions du GREF).
1993	*Tout-Monde* (novel) (Paris, Gallimard). Glissant is named honorary president of the International Parliament of Writers (Paris), of which he was one of the founding members. He is named doctor *honoris causa* by the University of the West Indies, first in Trinidad, then in Jamaica.
1994	He is named distinguished professor at the City University of New York Graduate Center. *Les Grands Chaos* (poems) (Gallimard, Paris).
1996	*Faulkner, Mississippi* (essay) (Paris Stock). *Poèmes complets, Introduction à une poétique du divers* (essay) (Gallimard, Paris).
1997	*Traité du Tout-Monde, Poétique IV* (Paris, Gallimard).
1998	Glissant marries Sylvie Sémavoine in New Jersey.
1999	*Sartorius. Le roman des Batoutos* (novel) (Paris, Gallimard).
2000	*Le Monde incréé, poétrie* (theatre) (Paris, Gallimard), which includes three plays: *Conte de ce que fut la tragédie d'Askia* (1963) *Parabole d'un moulin de la Martinique* (1975) *La Folie Celat* (1987).
2002	Creation of the Édouard Glissant Prize at the University of Paris-VIII (Vincennes) in collaboration with La maison de l'Amérique latine and, later, the Institut du Tout-Monde.
2003	*Ormerod* (novel) (Paris, Gallimard).

2004	Glissant is named doctor *honoris causa* by the University of Bologna, Italy.
2005	*La Cohée du Lamentin, Poétique V* (essay) (Paris, Gallimard).
2006	*Une nouvelle région du monde, Esthétique I* (essay) (Paris, Gallimard). Glissant founds the Institut du Tout-Monde in Paris. The French president Jacques Chirac asks for his participation in the founding of a National Center of Slavery.
2007	*La Terre magnétique, les errances de Rapa Nui, l'île de Pâques* (with Sylvie Séma) (Paris, Le Seuil). *Mémoires des esclavages* (Paris, Gallimard). *Quand les murs tombent. L'identité nationale hors-la-loi?* (pamphlet) with Patrick Chamoiseau (Paris, Galaade).
2008	*Les Entretiens de Baton Rouge*, interviews with Alexandre Leupin (Paris, Gallimard).
2009	*Philosophie de la Relation*, Paris, Gallimard. *L'intraitable beauté du monde, adresse à Barack Obama* (pamphlet) (Paris, Galaade). *Manifeste pour les produits de haute nécessité* (pamphlet) (Paris, Galaade).
2010	*Philosophie de la Relation, poésie en étendue* (essay), Paris Gallimard. *10 mai. Mémoires de la traite négrière, de l'esclavage et de leurs abolitions* (essay) (Paris, Galaade). *La terre, le feu, l'Eau et les Vents, une anthologie de la poésie du Tout-Monde* (poetry) (Paris, Galaade). *L'imaginaire des langues*, interviews with Lise Gauvin (Paris, Gallimard).
3 February 2011	Death in Paris.
2015	Glissant's archives are declared a national treasure by the French government and transferred to the National French Library (BNF).

Timeline established with the help of Professors Jean-Pierre Sainton and Raphaël Lauro.

Contents

Translator's Introduction	1
The Gardens in the Sands	5
The Cry of the World	7
Repetitions	21
Treatise on the Whole-World by Mathieu Béluse	27
Book 1	27
Book 2	33
Book 3	40
Waves and Backwashes	45
The Time of the Other	55
Writing	73
What Was Us, What Is Us	77
Punctuations	111
Objections to this 'Treatise' by Mathieu Béluse, and Reply	129
Measure, Immeasurability	137
The Town, Refuge for the Voices of the World	153

Translator's Introduction

Édouard Glissant was not only a thinker but also a novelist and poet, and the essays in *Treatise on the Whole-World* reflect this; not only do characters from the novels appear from time to time (and indeed the *Treatise* itself is presented as written by a fictional character), but much of the writing has a poetic quality that is quite different from the conventional style of the essay (as Glissant says: 'the poetics that have appeared in the world are gaily reinventing the genres, unrestrainedly mixing them up', p. 75). The book also contains two actual poems (pp. 138–9, p. 152). He invents new words whose meaning is not always clearly defined, and abstract discussion alternates with lyrical evocations of landscapes, cities or people ('You ask why I am jumping about like this, going from polished sentences to all kinds of jumbles of words?', p. 40). Repetition, also, has a positive rather than a negative value, because it is never exact: looking at the same idea from a slightly different angle can shed new light on it.

The fabric of the text thus echoes its core meaning: namely, the value it accords to *diversity*. This in itself of course is hardly original – although it was more so in the context of the French republican ideology in which Glissant was working – but he extends it far beyond the usual conventions of multiculturalism. Difference goes together with Relation, one of his main concepts, which he always capitalizes: all social groups, and indeed individuals, exist in Relation with other, different, groups. This is particularly true of the modern world, in which colonization and immigration have brought together in one place extremely different cultures and lifestyles. Universal or absolute values, and any kind of homogenization, are to be rejected. 'Creolization' is a key term here, and a key positive value: Glissant generalizes it from its usual designation of the racially mixed societies of the Caribbean and the Indian Ocean to *any* society in which different groups interact. Thus he distinguishes between 'atavistic' and 'composite', or creolized, cultures. The interaction associated with the latter produces new and constantly evolving, unpredictable configurations.

Unpredictability in general is, in his view, a major characteristic of our modern world, and one that we have to learn to accept. Similarly, he is totally opposed to the idea of the *system*, with its generalizing, mechanical predictability. He contrasts the system with what he calls the 'trace': a 'wandering that guides us' (p. 2) and is both a path that we can follow and the trace, in the conventional sense, that people leave behind of their culture.

The notion of *place* is important to the book as a whole. 'Place is crucial', as he says several times (e.g. p. 37); we are formed by the place that we live in. He reinvents the derogatory notion of the 'common-place' as a positive 'common place', i.e. a place that we have in common. But he also constructs an important and non-conflictual relation between the specificity of the place that one lives in and the world in general. This is the 'Whole-World', which is the world subjectively experienced in terms of relationality: as he says,

I call the Whole-World our universe as it changes and lives on through its exchanges and, at the same time, the 'vision' that we have of it. The world-totality in its physical diversity and in the representations that it inspires in us: so that we are no longer able to sing, speak or work based on our place alone, without plunging into the imagination of this totality (p. 108)

(This is the exact opposite of globalization, which is seen in entirely negative terms as suppressing difference.) A kind of variation on the Whole-World is the 'Chaos-World', which emphasizes not only the unpredictability of the world but also the clashes of different cultures.

All of this also impacts on our conception of personal identity, where Glissant borrows from the work of Gilles Deleuze and Félix Guattari to set up an opposition between the 'root' and the 'rhizome': i.e. 'root' identity which is completely self-sufficient versus identity as the 'rhizome' that reaches out to others and is constructed in relation to them.

A large part of the *Treatise* is devoted to questions of language, where once again Glissant urges his readers to celebrate the diversity of languages and, in particular, to protect those minority languages that are in danger of disappearing. While using my own language, I must always be aware of the existence of all the others: I can no longer write or speak 'monolingually'. (It is not clear how this difference might be perceptible to others.) The interest in language(s) also leads to a discussion of the practice, and the virtues, of translation (p. 20). And the theme of language also figures, of course, in the many discussions of writers that occur in the book. Glissant was extraordinarily well-read, and moves fluently between major modern French writers, those that are far less widely known, and the ancient 'founding' texts of not only European but also Asian and Arabic societies. But he is equally fascinated by the conspicuously modern phenomena of computing and audiovisual techniques and how these have completely re-set the relation between oral and written modes of language.

Throughout the *Treatise* there is also an impassioned concern with the world's poor, the dispossessed and the oppressed: in many ways this is very straightforward, but it links in with Glissant's overall promotion of relatedness and diversity, and gives these a more overtly political dimension. He is extremely scathing about multinational companies because of their exploitation of the poor – but also because he sees them, with 'their circumference everywhere and their centre nowhere' (p. 153), as the ultimate negation of the importance of place. He also insists that culture in general is necessarily political, and at one point argues (not entirely convincingly, in my view) that the main political conflicts of our time are to do with culture (p. 153). Two chapters are devoted to political figures: Nelson Mandela and Léopold Senghor (although the latter concentrates more on his writing than his political activities). And the section entitled 'Martinique' (pp. 141–5) is a very solid and detailed proposal for an ecological project to reclaim the island, while another section is devoted to the setting up of 'refuge towns' for persecuted writers (pp. 155–9).

More generally, history features prominently in the *Treatise*, especially in the section devoted to the European Middle Age (pp. 56–62), where Glissant focuses on the transition, as he sees it, from the multiplicity and diversity of the early medieval period to the beginnings of classicism with its emphasis on universality. But history also takes the far more personal form of his adolescent memories of the Second World War, the privations it imposed on the people of Martinique, and the 'dissidents' who clandestinely left the island to fight in the Resistance (pp. 29–31). Geography, also, is a significant theme in the frequent glorification of islands and archipelagos as contrasted with continents, and he comments briefly on the similarities and differences between science and artistic creation (p. 133).

The *Treatise* is thus extraordinarily wide-ranging in its subject matter, while at the same time linking its very varied topics together through a fairly small number of key concepts: the values of diversity and Relation are not only proclaimed but exemplified by the text itself. It is certainly one of the most challenging books that Glissant has written, but also one of the most rewarding.

Celia Britton

To Olivier Glissant
For the big and the little waves
For the big and the little tunes

✦ ✦ ✦

The Gardens in the Sands

(Theme for the essential dialogue with a poet)

The Gardens: The secret part of the poem, that solitude and grace that the storyteller keeps for himself. The place that he offers to the intuitive attention of She who reads omens, to the dissertations of the friend and the brother, in a fragile sharing.

The Sands: The drunken swirling of the world's engagements, where everyone chants and enchants. Suffering also all sufferings. The Sands are not infertile. They bring silence amidst all this noise round about.

The Cry of the World

We are told, and it is true, that everything is disorganized, confused, decrepit, madness is everywhere, the blood the wind. We see it and we live it. But it is the whole world that is speaking to you, through so many gagged voices.

Wherever you turn, there is desolation. But you still turn.

Doubtless we then bring to the co-operation of all knowledge, when we make ourselves share it, what each of us has long meditated or proclaimed, and, in my case, those few premonitions that have led me to write and that I have constantly transcribed, or betrayed through my inadequacy, in writing.

The thought of hybridity, of the trembling value not only of hybrid cultures but, going further, of cultures of hybridity, which perhaps save us from the limitations or the intolerances that lie in wait for us, and will open up for us new spaces of relation.

The mutual impact of the techniques or the mentalities of the oral and the written, and the inspirations that these techniques have breathed into our traditions of writing and our outbursts of voices, gestures and cries.

The slow erosion of the absolutes of History, as the histories of peoples who have been disarmed, dominated or sometimes are purely and simply disappearing but have nevertheless burst onto the scene of our common theatre, have finally met up and contributed to changing the whole representation that we had of History and its system.

The more and more evident workings of what I have called creolization, overtaking us, unpredictable, and so far away from the boring syntheses, already refuted by Victor Segalen,* that a moralizing thinking would have offered us.

The diffracted poetics of this Chaos-world that we share, on a level with and beyond so many conflicts and obsessions with death, and whose invariants we will have to discover.

The harmony and, just as persistent, the disharmonies that multilingualism generates in us, this new passion for our most secret voices and rhythms.

*

These are some of the echoes that have now resulted in our consenting to listen together to the cry of the world, knowing also that, as we listen, we understand that *from now on everyone can hear it.*
We do not always see, and usually we try not to see, the destitution of the world, in the forests of Rwanda and the streets of New York, in the underground workshops of Asia where the children do not grow up and the silent heights of the Andes, and in all the places of debasement, degradation and prostitution, and so many others that flash before our wide open eyes, but we cannot fail to admit that all this is making a noise, an unstoppable murmuring that we, without realizing it, mix into the mechanical, humdrum little tunes of our progress and our driftings.

Each one of us has his own reasons to listen to this cry, and these different approaches serve to change this sound of the world that we all, at the same time, hear where we are.

And these reasons, which we have seized on in the difficult passion of writing and creating, of living and struggling, are now becoming common places for us, that we are learning to share; but invaluable common places: against the disorders of the identitarian machines of which we are so often the prey, like for example the birthright, the purity of the race, the integrality, if not the integrity, of the dogma.

---

* Victor Segalen (1878–1919), an important influence on Glissant, was one of the first French thinkers to write about exoticism.

Our common places, even though today they are of no use, of absolutely no use against the concrete oppressions that stun the world, are nevertheless capable of changing the imagination* of human communities: it is through the imagination that we will ultimately conquer these derelictions that attack us, just as it already helps us, by shifting our sensibilities, to fight them.

This will be my first proposition: where systems and ideologies have failed, and without in any way giving up on the resistance or the fight that you must carry on in your particular place, let us extend the imagination by an infinite bursting forth and an infinite repetition of the themes of hybridity, multilingualism and creolization.

*

Those who meet up *here* always come from an 'over there', from the expanse of the world, and here they are, determined to bring to this 'here' the fragile knowledge that they have taken from over there. Fragile knowledge is not imperious science. We sense that we are following a trace.

So this is my second proposition:
That the thought of the *trace*, as opposed to systematic thought, acts as a wandering that guides us. We know that the trace is what puts us, all of us, wherever we come from, in Relation.
And for some people, over there, so far so near, right here, on the hidden face of the earth, the trace was lived as one of the places of survival. For example, for the descendants of the Africans transported into slavery into what would soon be called the New World, it was usually the only possible form of action.

*

---

* In English, 'the imaginary' is associated primarily with its use in the work of Lacan and Althusser, where it has a rather different meaning. I have therefore preferred to translate 'l'imaginaire' here as 'imagination', which should be understood not as the faculty of imagining but as a kind of distinctive repertoire of images that orientate one's thinking, in the sense in which we speak of 'the Romantic imagination', 'the Puritan imagination', etc.

(A whole chunk of reality, seized from a recalcitrant past, redistributed into every corner of life, repeated in each book:)

The trace is to the route as rebellion to the command, jubilation to the garrotte.

Those Africans transported to the Americas carried with them, over the Great Seas, the trace of their gods, of their customs, of their languages. Faced with the implacable disorder of the settler, they had the genius, arising from the suffering they endured, to make these traces fertile, creating – better than syntheses – outcomes that no-one expected.

The Creole languages are traces, opening up across the seas of the Caribbean or the Indian Ocean. Jazz music is a trace that has been recomposed and spread all over the world. And all the different kinds of music of this Caribbean and the Americas.

When these deported slaves marooned in the woods, leaving the Plantation, the traces they followed were not those of self-abandonment or despair, but nor were they those of pride or egotism. And they did not weigh on the new land as irreparable stigmas.

When we – I mean the Antilleans – rush into these traces of our undervalued histories, it is not in order to quickly outline a model of humanity that we would then oppose, in a ready-made fashion, to those other models that are forcibly imposed on us.

The trace is not an unfinished path where one stumbles helplessly, nor an alley closed on itself, bordering a territory. The trace goes into the land, which will never again be a territory. The trace is an opaque way of experiencing the branch and the wind: of being oneself, derived from the other. It is the truly disordered sand of utopia.

Trace thought enables us to move away from the strangulations of the system. It thus refutes the extremes of possession. It cracks open the absolute of time. It opens onto these diffracted times that human communities today are multiplying among themselves, through conflicts and miracles.

It is the violent wandering of the shared thought.

(Thus for me, from cry to word, from folk tale to poem, from *Soleil de la conscience* to the *Poétique du divers*, this same momentum.)*

---

* *Soleil de la concience* (1956) was Glissant's first collection of essays, and *Introduction à une Poétique du divers* (1996) immediately precedes the *Traité du Tout-monde*.

*

If we abandon systematic thoughts, it is because we have realized that they have imposed, here and there, an absolute of Being, which was profundity, magnificence, and limitation.

*

So many communities under threat today have only the alternatives of, on the one hand, the tearing apart of their being, identitarian anarchy, war between nations and dogmas, and, on the other, a Roman peace imposed by force, an empty neutrality imposed on everything by an all-powerful, totalitarian, well-meaning Empire.

Are we reduced to these impossible choices? Do we not have the right and the means to live another dimension of humanity? But how?

*

As much as ever, masses of Negroes are threatened and oppressed because they are Negroes, Arabs because they are Arabs, Jews because they are Jews, Muslims because they are Muslims, Indians because they are Indians, and so on through the infinite diversities of the world. This litany is indeed never-ending.

The idea of identity as a single root provides the measure according to which these communities were enslaved by others, and in the name of which a number of them led their liberation struggles.

But could we not propose, against the single root that kills everything around it, an extension of the root into a rhizome,* which opens up Relation? It is not rootless: but it does not take over its surroundings.

Onto the imagination of single-root identity, let us graft this imagination of rhizome-identity.

---

* Glissant borrows this term from *Mille Plateaux*, Gilles Deleuze and Félix Guattari (1980).

Against Being, which asserts itself, let us show being, which attaches itself.*

Let us challenge both the returns of the nationalist repressed and the sterile universal peace of the Powerful.

In a world where so many communities find themselves mortally denied the right to any identity, it is paradoxical to propose the imagination of an identity-relation, an identity-rhizome. I believe however that this is indeed one of the passions of these oppressed communities, to believe in this moving beyond identity and to carry it along with their sufferings.

No need to bleat about a humanist vocation to understand this, quite simply.

*

I call *Chaos-World* the current clash of so many cultures set ablaze, pushing each other away, disappearing, but still persisting, sleeping or transforming themselves, slowly or at lightning speed: these bursts, these explosions whose principle or economy we have not yet begun to understand, and whose trajectory we cannot predict. The Whole-World, which is totalizing, is not (for us) total.

And I call *Poetics of Relation* this possibility of the imagination that leads us to conceive of the elusive 'worldness' of such a Chaos-World, at the same time as it allows us to pick up some detail from it, and in particular to sing the praises of our place, unfathomable and irreversible. Imagination is not a dream, or the emptiness of an illusion.

*

You will have realized that one of the traces of this Poetics goes through the common place. How many people at the same time, in opposite or convergent situations, are thinking the same things, asking the same questions. Everything is in everything, without being forcibly mixed together. You come up with an idea, they greedily take it up, it is theirs. They proclaim it. They claim it. This is what characterizes the common place. It mobilizes our imaginations better than any system of ideas, but

---

* Where Glissant distinguishes in the phenomenological sense between 'l'être' and 'l'étant' I have translated these terms as 'Being' and 'being' respectively.

only as long as you are looking out for it. Here are some that concern the connection between cultures in world-wide Relation.

For the first time, the semi-totality of human cultures are entirely and simultaneously put in contact and in effervescent reaction with one another.
(But there are still some closed places and some different *times*.)

The worldness, or totality, of the phenomenon defines its character: the exchanges between cultures are not subtle, the adoptions or rejections are fierce.
(The law of basic pleasure, individual or collective, reinforced or maintained by the mechanisms of power and persuasion, presides over both adoption and rejection.)

For the first time also, the peoples are completely conscious of the exchange. The television of everything intensifies these kinds of connections.
(If there are surreptitious echoes, they are quickly spotted.)

The interrelations are strengthened or weakened at a speed that is barely conceivable.
(In other words this speed gives us light in the frightening immobility of so many dizzying changes in the world.)

Whole groups of influences (the dominant ones) take shape, in some cases leading to a generalized standardization.
(Do not think that you can fight this just by exaggerating your separateness.)

Relation implies no *legitimizing* transcendence. If the places of power are invisible, the Centres of Law impose themselves nowhere.
(Also, Relation has no morality: it does not choose. And it does not have to define anything that would be its 'content'. Relation, because it is totalizing, is intransitive.)

The interrelations proceed largely through fractures and ruptures. They are even perhaps of a fractal nature: this is why our world is a chaos-world.
Their general economy and their momentum are those of *creolization*.

*

From these Archipelagos that I live in, risen up among so many others, I propose to you that we should think about this creolization.

*

An unstoppable process, which mixes the substance of the world, which joins up and changes the cultures of today's humanities. What Relation gives us to imagine, creolization has given us to experience.

Creolization does not lead to loss of identity, to a dilution of the being. It does not imply renunciation of the self. It suggests the distance (the going away) from the overwhelming fixities of Being.

Creolization is not something that disturbs a given culture from the inside, even if we know that a number of cultures have been and will be dominated, assimilated, brought to the brink of disappearance. Beyond these often disastrous conditions, it acts to maintain relations between two or more cultural 'zones', brought together in a meeting place, just as a Creole language functions on the basis of differentiated linguistic 'zones' to take from them its new substance.

It soon becomes clear that although there have always been places of creolization (cultural hybridities), that which interests us today concerns the world-totality, once this totality has been realized (mainly through the action of expanding Western cultures, that is to say, through the work of colonizations). Relation feeds the imagination, which has still to be imagined, of a creolization that is now generalized and does not weaken.

Creolization is unpredictable, it is never fixed, or stopped, or inscribed in essences or absolutes of identity. To accept that the being changes while remaining is not to veer towards an absolute. What remains in the changing or the change or the exchange is perhaps first of all the inclination or the daring to change.

I offer you the word creolization, to signify that unpredictability of completely new outcomes, that saves us from believing in an essence or the rigidity of exclusiveness.

*

This shimmering of the being splashes over into my way of using language: our common condition here is multilingualism.

From now on I write in the presence of all the world's languages, in the poignant nostalgia of their threatened future. I understand that there is no point in trying to learn as many of them as possible: multilingualism is not quantitative. It is one of the modes of the imagination. In the language I use to express myself, and even if it is the only one I possess, I no longer write in a monolingual fashion.

'Maintaining' languages, helping to save them from wearing out and disappearing, constitutes this imagination of which there is so much to say. Let us not believe that one language could, tomorrow and with no trouble, become universal: it would soon perish, under the very code that its generalized use would have brought about. Anglo-American pidgin first and foremost threatens the surprises, the leaps, the organic, energetic life, the precious weaknesses and the secret retreats of the English and American and Canadian and Australian, etc., language. Simplification, which facilitates exchanges, immediately distorts them.

*

The first meeting of the International Writers' Parliament, in Strasbourg in 1993, was not completely polyglot, but it was certainly multilingual.

It was not the first time that writers and intellectuals tried to come together in a conference or an assembly; history provides us with illustrious examples.

It was perhaps not the first time that people tried to restore the meaning of this word Parliament, not a place where one is elected, one votes and decides, but a place where one speaks [parle].

But it was the first time that such a Parliament also proposed to *listen*, quite simply – to what? We have already said: to the cry of the world.

Not theories, ideologies or powers – not a system or an idea of the world – but the huge entanglement, where one neither sacrifices oneself in lamentations nor gets carried away with hopes. The word of the world crying out, where the voice of every community is heard. The accumulation of common places, of displaced cries, of mortal silences, where one can understand that the power of States is not our true motive, and agree that our truths are not linked to power.

*

(And now having evoked languages under threat, *langages* on the way out, I come back to another of my torments and repeat something I have already said, like an echo streaked into a piece of chalk which in turn is carved from fragile limestone.* This is to magnify the openings that the exercise of translation creates between languages and *langages*):

Translation is like an art of flight, in other words, so eloquently, a renunciation that accomplishes.

Renunciation when the poem, transcribed into another language, has given up the greater part of its rhythm, its secret structures, its assonances, these accidents that are the chance and the permanence of writing.

We must accept these losses, and this renunciation is the part of oneself that in any poetics we give up to the other.

The art of translation teaches us the thinking of evasion, the practice of the trace, which, as against systematic thought, points the way to the uncertain, the threatened, which come together and strengthen us. Yes, translation, art of the approach and the light touch, is a way of frequenting the trace.

Against the absolute limitation of the concepts of 'Being', the art of translation brings together the 'being'. To trace in languages is to gather together the unpredictable in the world. Translation does not consist of reducing something to transparency, nor of course in joining up two systems of transparency.

Hence, this other proposition, which the practice of translation suggests: to set against the transparency of models the open opacity of irreducible existences.

*

I claim for everyone the right to *opacity*, which is not the same as closing oneself off.

It is a means of reacting against all the ways of reducing us to the false clarity of universal models.

I do not have to 'understand' anyone, individual, community, people – i.e. to 'take them with me' at the cost of smothering them, of losing them

---

*   English has no equivalent for the distinction between 'langue' and 'langage', which is an important element in Glissant's discussion of language use. He uses 'langage' to denote the speaker's subjective attitude to the 'langue' (French, English, Creole, etc.) that s/he uses.

in a boring totality that I would be in charge of - in order to agree to live with them, to build with them, to take risks with them.

Let opacity, whether it be ours for the other or maybe the other's for us, not close down in obscurantism or apartheid; let it be a celebration, not a terror. Let the right to opacity, whereby Diversity will best be preserved and acceptance strengthened, be a lamp watching over our poetics.

*

All of this, that I have briefly recalled, serves only to open up the trace to other utterances. Here I am appealing to conjoined poetics. Our actions in the world will remain sterile if we do not change, as best we can, the imagination of the human communities that we constitute.

Proof of this for me is the people that Matta* assembled at the entrance to that Writers' Parliament, in Strasbourg in 1993. You were welcomed by the cry of a whole crowd. A people of statues, where the Inca headdress covered the Egyptian toga, where the sari from Africa was draped over the Inuit pose, where the mouldings of bronze or copper, yellow breathing and violet suffering, supported all kinds of stylized forms, recognizable and intermixed, coming from all over the world, springing from so many of the beauties of the world. These works were hybrid, their architecture revealed diversity, mobilized by an artist into an unhoped-for result. Yes. These statues brought together this cry.

A people that speaks like this is a country that shares.

---

* Roberto Matta (1911–2002) was a surrealist painter from Chile.

Archipelagic thinking suits the pace of our worlds. It has their ambiguity, their fragility, their drifting. It accepts the practice of the detour, which is not the same as fleeing or giving up. It recognizes the range of the imaginations of the Trace, which it ratifies. Does this mean giving up on self-government? No, it means being in harmony with the world as it is diffracted in archipelagos, precisely, these sorts of diversities in spatial expanses, which nevertheless rally coastlines and marry horizons. We become aware of what was so continental, so thick, weighing us down, in the sumptuous systematic thought that up until now has governed the History of human communities, and which is no longer adequate to our eruptions, our histories and our no less sumptuous wanderings. The thinking of the archipelago, the archipelagos, opens these seas up to us.

Even from the point of view of identity, the scope of the poem results from the search, wandering and often anxious, of conjunctions of forms and structures that allow an idea of the world, expressed in the poem's own place, to meet (or not) other ideas of the world. Writing draws the common places of the real together to found a rhetoric. Michel Leiris did this in his work. Maurice Roche also, in a different way.* Identity does not proclaim itself, in this domain of literature and forms of expression: it is operational. The proportion of the means of expression and their adequacy are stronger than mere proclamation. Advertising one's identity is nothing but uttering a threat if it is not also the measure of a way of speaking. When on the contrary we point to and inform the forms of our speaking, our identity is no longer based on an essence, it leads to Relation.

---

* Michel Leiris (1901–1990) was a surrealist poet and ethnographer; Maurice Roche (1924–1997) was a prose writer from the 1960s to the 1990s. Both were friends of Glissant.

✦ ✦ ✦

Repetitions

The movements of the discovery and colonization of the world first of all brought into contact atavistic cultures, which had long been established each in its own belief and on its own territory.

Atavistic cultures, because they were legitimized by a Genesis, a Creation of the world, which inspired them and of which they made a Myth, the hub of their collective existence.

It is certainly a privilege to have direct access to the Sacred, to speak to one's God, to be entrusted with his intentions. As a result any community or culture that thus generated a Genesis was determined to make of it a lesson for everyone. Through an absolutely legitimate succession of filiations (that cannot be challenged), it attaches itself to that first day of Creation, and thus asserts its Right on the land that it occupies, which becomes its territory. Filiation and legitimacy are the two pillars of that sort of divine Right of property, at least as far as European cultures are concerned.

The cultures of the Arabic countries, black African countries and Amerindian countries are also atavistic. With, however, all kinds of nuances in their approach to the divine, in the imagined modes of Creation, and consequently in their claims to the land they occupy.

The coming into contact of these atavistic cultures in the spaces of colonization has given rise in places to composite cultures and societies, which have not generated any Genesis (adopting Creation Myths from elsewhere), for the reason that their origin is not lost in darkness, that it is obviously of a historical rather than mythical order. The Genesis of the Creole societies of the Americas is founded in a different obscurity, that of the belly of the slave ship. This is what I call a digenesis.

Acclimatize yourself to the idea of digenesis, get used to its example, and you will leave behind the impenetrable demands of exclusive uniqueness.

Composite societies relate to the sacred or the divine only indirectly, one might almost say by proxy. Their sects, for example, combine surprising syntheses of Genesis, borrowing from everywhere, in an exaggerated fashion. When, as in Haiti or Brazil, one encounters religions whose inspiration is from Dahomey, their impulse is atavistic and their rites composite. But the societies in question have the advantage of not being constrained by thousands of years of customs and undecipherable taboos, whose weight would be crushing.

Most of the convulsions of our times are determined by this context: atavistic cultures fighting each other to the death over their respective legitimacies, or quarrelling over the legitimate right to extend their territory. Or imposing this legitimacy on other cultures of the world. Composite cultures contesting old atavistic cultures over the last remains of their past legitimacy.

These propositions, even if they have sometimes been copied by others, must be repeated, for as long as they have not been heard.

*

Creolization is the putting into contact of several cultures or at least several elements of distinct cultures, in a particular place in the world, resulting in something new, completely unpredictable in relation to the sum or the simple synthesis of these elements.

One can predict the outcome of a cross-breeding, but not of a creolization. Both of these, in the atavistic universe, were thought to produce a dilution of being, a bastardization. Another unexpected fact is that this prejudice is slowly dying out, even if it remains strong in immobile, barricaded places.

The idea of atavistic belonging helps people to endure destitution and strengthens their courage in fighting servitude and oppression. In a composite society where the elements of culture are hierarchized, where one of them is made inferior compared to the others, the natural and the only possible reaction is to valorize this element in an atavistic manner, in a search for equilibrium, for certainty and permanence.

Could a homeless black American camping in cardboard boxes on an icy New York pavement accept the idea of creolization? He knows that his race and the singularity of his race for the Other have a great deal to do with the definition of his state.

Could the Amerindian societies threatened with extinction have defended themselves in the name of creolization, when the very mechanism that contributed, at least in the first instance, to their de-culturation seemed to be no different from creolization?

But that is what is at stake. We will not be able to untangle the contradictions of the Americas or the convulsions of the Whole-World until we have resolved in our imaginations the quarrel of the atavistic and the composite, of single root identity and relation-identity.

*

The United States of America for instance is a multi-ethnic society but one in which the interchange of ethnicities, which should have been the norm for such multiplicity, hardly ever happens. Three isolating factors are in operation here:

– the ancient oppositions and the traditions of conflict between the religions that came from Europe, whose impact on the new situation can be more or less obscure, more or less innocent;

– the long struggle against the Amerindian nations (the Conquest of the West) and their almost complete extermination;

– the deportation of slaves from Africa (the Slave Trade) whose repercussions are still visible.

In all these cases, oppressors and oppressed needed to refer themselves back to their ethnicity as a uniqueness or a value, and it is perhaps more convincing or efficacious that these ethnic singularities be maintained: with the result that history, at least up until the present, ends up in this apparent contradiction: a multiethnic society that is prey to interethnic isolation.

A country of multiculturalism, the United States is not – or not yet – a country of creolization. The latter, which is developing, needs general agreement, which is difficult to obtain.

*

Finally, the question that should be implicitly inscribed in this debate is the following: would a modern theory of multiculturalism not allow us, in reality, just to camouflage the old atavistic reflex more effectively, by presenting the relation between cultures or communities, within a large entity like the United States, as a reassuring juxtaposition and not as an unpredictable (and dangerous) creolization?

These propositions must be repeated, until they are at least heard.

The *Street of Mounting Desire* ends up in the middle of the one hundred and nine rivers that fall from the casuarinas and the wild mango trees. There, we can taste the bitter mauby. The *Street of the Green Cave* widens out, swells out its canefields until they reach the park of the sea, where the bulls are kept. One can hardly see on the horizon the smoky little lights where the zombies dance their dance, ah! all along the *Street of Come Back Here*. We go fishing there at night, guarded by the mosquitoes. These streets make up an archipelago, the archipelago makes foam, we inhabit the foam. Big and strong, and hypocritical, The *Street fouté-fè* offers itself to tourists. In its crossing, the *Street of the Fine Evening Smoking* fans the flames of its volcanoes, like Man Tine smoking her pipe, her eyes closed. We know that street can also be called 'via': we plunge into the *Via dei umiliati*, in the direction of the *Via dei malcontenti*. At the end of the day we run to make our bows, *Street of the Mad Virgins*. Then to do our washing, *Street of the Crouching Old Men*. We overflow into the entrance, covered in grass and culverts, of the *Street of the End of the World*.

Treatise on the Whole-World
by Mathieu Béluse

Book 1

The countries I live in are scattered like stars into archipelagos. They join together the times of their bursting forth. When we come across an impenetrable piece of time, an unbreakable rock – which we also call a 'bi' – here we are in front of this 'bi' of time, we are not disorientated by it, we go around this obscurity, we tread the slightest ravine or the smallest cape, until we can enter into it. The brilliance of the times, just like the brilliance of the weather, does not lead us astray, in our countries.

We had known that we could live, not out of time, but without it, at least without the need to organize it into regular lines or divide it into permanent sections. The time as it passed was not lost, it was simply devoid of life (and yet we remembered everything, in a muddle of appearances) and life exploded not outside but across time, in these gatherings of sunshine or rain, of Lent or of overflowing rivers, where with our little nets and a lot of bubbles we caught the big black fish with square heads, or raked over the depths of pools to hunt down the water, under the enormous eyes of the jowly toads.

What we never failed to do was to think about faraway countries. As though the image of spatial expanse corresponded to our lack of concern for duration in time. In the unbreakable piece of time that my childhood still represents for me, the life of distant countries was amazing. That really helped us to learn the list of the eighty-nine departments of France that we had to recite, chanting, with the main towns and the number of inhabitants falling like drumbeats at the end of the line. Many of us had never seen or thought about anything from France, even if we enjoyed French flour, French onions and French butter, whenever we could get hold of a bit of them.

Man Thimotée and her lover never stopped coming back together and splitting up again. They would hold conversations that we could never decipher. They spoke to each other through symbols and parables, as though their relationship was made for the folk tale that we turned it into, and their lives, when they were apart, no longer had any shape.

She would shout: 'I am Brazil in embers [en braise] and I have glowed [brasillé] in all winds. You do not know the heat of the steam on my skin and on my continents.'

He would call her: 'Halt, mademoiselle! Stay there and repeat. Consider China and chinoiserie and the robe of the mandarin. I am the divination and the life'.

She would sing: 'We will pull the cord all around [tout autour] all the days in the finery [atours] of the surroundings [alentour]'.

He would pray: 'Oh God make the trace to have traced, make the world to have summoned [que le monde a mandé], and then that the sun rises and sets on this rope'.

ManTimothée sold fritters and cane syrup, locchios, mauby and holy grass. Her lover fished. They imagined the faraway countries. One day they were found dead in their shack, wearing their Sunday best, lying on their bed, no-one could understand why. You never understand bitterness or death. Was it in 1965, the year of the birth of Jérôme? This is what in books they call a novel.

*

The reeds laid out to dry for making straw hats and fans, the persimmon trees in the cool shade, the clumps of coffee plants in pink and brown tunes, the joining together of the sugar cane plants that harass you with their thorns and their suns, this is just a piece of that time that we did not know and did not know that it had already caught us in its snare and its rocks.

Because the thing that was called World War II was roaming around us. Ever since the world first cried out, that is, since these drubbings of rocks began to attack us, we have waged war, World or colonial, where they have used us as cannon-fodder. And if you say that, simply that you have fought in all these wars, they immediately delegate some official, with the grimace of the accomplice or the slug [limace] of the transmuted, who reproaches you: 'Ah! You like talking about wars …' But we did not decide. We fought, if one can say that.

And so, the World War evaporated around us. So much so that we too learnt to count mechanically: Before, During and After the war. Which was a way of gathering into a pile these rocks of time that were tumbling down all around, so that at least they would stop attacking us.

The World War did not affect us directly. It had surrounded us with thunderous great boats, this was the Mericans, occasionally visible on the horizon. We were left there with all our embittered conflicts with one another, under the vigilant eyes of the occupiers: vigilant in plundering what little food remained in the country to nourish a voracious fleet. A stretch of land surrounded by sea, that is, by cruisers and torpedo boats, encourages you to imagine distant places. Those of us who left to join the Resistance, across the St Lucia Channel in the south or that of Dominica in the north, the Fanons and Manvilles* and others, 'on a frail skiff' on a moonless night, had hardly escaped the Petainist patrol boats, and long before humbly greeting the customs officers in the ports of Roseau or Castries or being hoisted aboard one of those big boats, when they started to realize that the faraway countries were not what they had imagined. Perhaps quite simply because the fisherman who smuggled them across had never told them that these Channels to the south or north were so hard to cross.

So the great majority of the rest of us, who stayed there becalmed, were dying from something that was not quite famine, on heaps of sugar cane and therefore of red sugar, and on guns and thunderclaps and veritable rivers of rum, which the *békés*** were storing while they waited for the sea to be open.

We know that hunger makes you see into the distance. That is, when it is not definitive, when it has not looted all life around it, and you still have a few unripe green bananas that you have saved from the greed of the sailors and buried behind your shack to escape from the requisitions.

Imagine what we imagined then. An immobile field of sparks far away from the lands, where people ran without getting out of breath, worked without getting tired, ate without running out of food, we hardly needed to consult the Senegalese infantrymen garrisoned in the country to paint a picture of what Senegal was, nor to question the Corsican adjutants of the Colonial army to see exactly what Corsica was. If a civil servant of the

---
* Frantz Fanon, the well-known writer and activist; Marcel Manville was also active in the Resistance, leaving Martinique to fight with De Gaulle.
** The white settlers in the French Caribbean.

general Government revealed that he was from the Cévennes, or if people were blabbering about the Mericans and their country, where there is lots of oil, fat and beef and apparently not much pork, we could start another round and convoke the inhabitants of the Cévennes as much as we liked, and the Mericans no less than we had to.

Alfonse Patraque (not to be confused with the policeman Alphonse Tigamba)* had fallen madly in love with a 'matador'** from St Lucia. Life was already impossible for her, having entered Martinique on the quiet, and finding herself under a Vichy government, while she was English. We called people from St Lucia, black and white and Indian and Chinese, the English. Désira had not had time to organize her return home, and now it was too late, she had been blocked by the arrival of the French fleet, the *Béarn*, the *Surcouf*, and the *Émile Bertin*, who had disastrously entered the Baie des Flamands, fleeing both the German ships and the American torpedo boats. And now, she had this big upset in her existence. It seems that Alfonse had taken advantage of the situation, with a bit of singing, a lot of excited talking, to get to what he thought was just a little conquest of no importance. But then it had exploded in his body, and after that he floated across space, just repeating: 'My friends, my friends!'

Désira took advantage of this. She forced him, quite simply, to organize a crossing of the St Lucia Channel. It was simple, she told him: 'Promise me that you will do it, or else I'm going down to the Port this evening.' He retreated, exclaiming 'Yes, yes!' But none of the fishermen would take those two, they didn't have enough cash. They shouted to Alfonse: 'So, we've heard you want to go and join the Resistance?' He explained: 'No, no, it's not the country calling me, it's the Lord of love'. He exhausted all the possibilities, sailing boats, rowing boats, yalls, and even perhaps a little motorboat that went back and forth between Marin and Fort-de-France.

What was it that had exploded in his body? He realized that the storm had broken the first time he had put his hand on Désira's body, in this shack made of slates fitted in between poles of old wood, and she had pushed it away, because she wanted to take the lead. Ever since then, Alfonse had been feeling out of sorts; he wandered about in himself, searching for what it was that had come gushing out of him.

He found a big raft, the kind that was used for fishing oysters, and he equipped it just as a real amateur or a real fishing captain would have

---

* A character in Glissant's novel *Malemort* (1975).
** The term 'matador' is used of strong, self-reliant or aggressive women in Martinique.

done, with sails, oars, rudder, storage cabin. At the time, he would hiss as though in confidence (the authorities must not be alerted): 'I want to see the world, how it turns, and how it snows and makes ice, and how it burns.' And he did see it. After crossing the Channel, which was a panic-stricken rush, his body heaving on oars and ropes, the fight of a hero against the zombie winds and the evil spells of the waves, they were greeted at dawn by police from Castries who had come looking for them: they separated Désira and Alfonse, he was put into the regiment of the Antilles-Guyane which was fighting a German fortress in Bordeaux and (without even having the time to size up or rediscover whatever it was that had throbbed inside him so terribly) he died there from German shrapnel, ten minutes before the fortress was officially taken.

Ten years later, I met another Désira, but I was never blessed to know Alfonse's torment. I took things as they never came, and I was always ready for the pluperfect of the future. Men are always afraid, that is what keeps them safe. But I don't want to hide beneath generalities what belongs to me alone.

'Look', she said, 'the Amazonian forest, which is shrinking on its people and relentlessly counts those who fall, and its trees uprooted at the same time, a life a tree, a tree a life, cleared away. The forest of Zaire, a concentration camp, covered in mass graves, traversed by walking skeletons. They evaporate there, who could find their dust? We think about it, we think about it, and then we move on to something else. We say that the forests are the lungs of the earth. And so how can a forest cover such nights? How does it not shift these mismatches made by men? Ah! I wish I could tell you that I feel beautiful'.

Book 2

That is what she used to say. It is because she was capable of living here and over there, in several places at once, in several times, yesterday, tomorrow, and so she was afraid. We like to cherish our loves and our certainties in a place well lined with fabrics or leaves, soft and sweet. The idea of wandering seems to us vagrancy of feeling and moral laxity. To explore elsewhere frightens us, because we do not burn with the need to conquer and we do not see why we should go off rambling everywhere. Our imageries of the world were enough for us, they raved in us and for us, without our having to go and see. And so I was afraid, without realizing it, of a woman who could suddenly rush you off into places, without you being able turn off along the way. We men, black roosters and skinflints in huts, sense and feel that in the unhappiness that has always been their lot, the women of our countries have steered the boat of dreams and held the ropes of revolt and action and suffering, that we cautiously walked round, trying not to pull too hard on the rope. Such is their power. We resent it perhaps but, while we go on bragging as usual, it makes us really anxious.

We are also afraid of the unpredictable and do not know how to reconcile it with a possible concern to build, that is, to draw up plans. It will take time to learn this new way of moving into tomorrow: expecting uncertainty and preparing for what can only be guessed at.

But the women are not afraid of the unpredictable.

They are not allowed to see or touch the Gods but, better than any of the officials of the rite, they sense them. They show the way ahead and are able to prophesy; in modern parlance they are shrinks, they are the shattered spies of the unforeseeable.

I had already experienced this kind of division. I had known Oriamé* in what we call the Old Country, which is not, no monsieur, France, but the lands of Africa.

She lived in a town whose name escapes me, the names of towns in this far-off time indicated the function of the place or the colour of the ramparts or their situation: if they were on the edge of the forest or if they planted in the savannah their walls of dried mud or their round towers reflected in rivers wider than the sea. But the sea was far away and those who lived

---

* A symbolic character who first appears in Glissant's novel *Tout-monde* (1993).

near it had no idea what it was transporting away, protected as it was by fierce surf and merciless sandbars.

In this far away time, there was no time, except that which goes from the middle of the night to the middle of the day.

It was claimed that Oriamé the obscure was born in a shack where three women lived and where a blacksmith had spent the night, one night. In this darkness chosen at random, he had given birth. That is to say, the mother of Oriamé had vanished into that night, she had not appeared.

The blacksmith had not deigned to build his shack in the area, and nor did he want to work on the masks and the forms of our gods, perhaps he knew other ones, more powerful and more fortunate. He had made tools for everyone, without exception, without forgetting the very youngest boys still living with their mothers, and then he went away, as though he had suddenly died, leaving behind him only this collection of billhooks, machetes and all sorts of other tools, without counting the imminent arrival of Oriamé, of whom he was unaware. Relieved of the weight of the metals he had brought with him to us, he went off to rejoin the company of the ancestors and the gods, with whom he had a fixed appointment, but outside any known time, under the branches of a baobab or a silk-cotton tree or an acajou.

Oriamé's mother dedicated her to the Lord, master of all lives, who was called Askia, who sat in public on the backs of his prostrated slaves, carried out raids all over the land, then shut himself up in the innermost room of his big houses. All the lords were called Askia. In this far-off time people did not know, although it was coming soon, that the slaves were much more than slaves, that they were money, in property and wealth, they did not know what money was.

Oriamé, daughter of chance, dedicated to Lord Askia. Or else, princess born of such distant legends, and who refused him. She dies, by the hand of a plotting minister, thrown into a gulf surrounded by log wood trees. No, she is seized by a column of slave traders marching towards the sea, she throws herself into the depths of the sea from the bridge of the *Rose-Marie*, a slave ship. The ship's lieutenant, who wanted to keep her for himself, tells himself he has had a great loss. At the same time, two of the men shut up in the hold, two maniacs, two men possessed, are fighting for her, without noticing that she has jumped overboard, without even noticing that they are being taken, to where? Slaves in their chains, free men in all their hatred. No, no. She loved me, Lord Askia. Of course I did not realize I was African, Africa is not really Africa in other people's eyes until its conquest, I was a wanderer able to wear our masks, and Lord Askia did not condescend to have me in his regiments – nor that I was going to be Antillean, used to the splitting of my self and to running through time. She loved me, Lord Askia. But I know that all this is delusion and vertigo.

Oriamé had no inclination, given her destiny, to love anyone, lord or suitor.

After that, I entered a tale, which you call a novel. More surprised by this entrance than to have known, long ago, a princess who was said to be obscure. A tale, therefore a virtual world. I lived there according to laws that are scarcely decipherable. Wild speed carried me away. At every moment, crazy swerves into crossroads and turnings opened up unfathomable spaces. The colours shattered into pieces, but that was how they rambled on in their *langages*. The time for living was the same as the time for dying. The instant was identical to the duration.

At the same time, I am leading another life, supposedly real. I am perhaps 'he who occupies himself in the contemplation of a green stone', as the poet of Îlet-les-feuilles* says. And so I am vacant. Hurled into life. I go through my day, I carry out my tasks. We live together, Marie Celat and I, we have never got married, don't tell me that I am going back over stories already told. How much energy does it take to dig into a single story. There is only ever a single story. The truth is that I discover how much the life that is said to be real is mixed in with the virtuality of the tale, or the novel. In the tale is told, although very elliptically, the life-and-death of our two children, Patrice and Odono. The story-teller saw fit to make public something that in any case everyone in the country knows. It is also true that at one point in his story he made me die, or almost. A life-enhancing experience. When the times of the tale are mixed up like this with the times of life, it is the best way of staying there, suspended in the middle of a clear spell in the forest. The clear spell is not the name of the sun coming out after rain, it is a clearing, where the weather is sometimes bad. Patrice crashed in an accident, motorbike against truck, Odono got caught between two masses of seawater divided by a current. Or perhaps

---

* i.e. Saint-John Perse.

it's the other way around, sometimes I confuse the circumstances of each. As if the primordial waters and the brutal technology had got together to break the trace of filiation.

The fact remains that I share this pain (more terrible than if it had struck me alone) with Marie Celat, whom everyone here calls Mycéa.* Mycéa is the most dangerous of prophetesses. Out of all this momentum of the world as it prepares itself for us, as also this great white hole from which we have come, she has created the pretext of her existence. If I were not afraid of indulging in the worst possible sense of the common place, I would say that Marie Celat is an avatar, perhaps sacred, or cursed, of Oriamé. She has to throw herself in, every time, gulf or depths of the sea. She tells herself that this disposition is the only one that she has transmitted to her children, and that they followed it almost immediately, until they accomplished it in sudden death. As for me, I tell myself over and over again: what do I care about filiation, what I want is my children.

Is that what time is, for us? This repetition, from Oriamé to Mycéa? The same way of arching their bodies, but with their feet planted firmly in the ground, the same slight disdain of the lip when she shouts at you all at once such implacably organized speeches. The same beauty, black and red, with violet shadows, a beauty fiercely unaware of itself and which refuses to be recognized.

Don't say that I have looked for Oriamé in Mycéa, that is just stupid. No absolute of pain resembles another absolute of pain. Do women look, in the man that they are with, for a reflection of the one that was there yesterday? Could I say that Mycéa knew me in the life of the Old Country? Indeed, my life in the tale has joined my life, the only recourse I have been able to find against this delusion is to put this ubiquity into precepts and formulas, to scrape and hoe everything around it, in the hope that this writing preserves me (the artifices of the *langage* I adopt acting as a barrier) from listening to what is stirring beneath.

Some people cannot imagine the world, they rack their brains, but the world does not come out to spread itself in front of them. Those for whom it hurts to think about it, they too force it into these formulas that I use, for the same (un)reason that we do not know how to get hold of it. It governs our place, our narrative, our wandering.

---

* One of Glissant's most important characters, who appears in virtually all his novels.

1. The Place. It is crucial, because one cannot replace it, nor go around it.

But if you wish to profit in this place that has been given to you, reflect on the fact that from now on all the places of the world are meeting up, as far as the cosmic spaces.
You must no longer project into elsewhere the uncontrollable aspects of your place.

Think of the spatial expanse and its mystery, so accessible. Do not leave your shore for a voyage of discovery or conquest.
Let the voyage take over.

Or rather, leave from elsewhere and come back up here, where your house and your source of water open up.
Run to the imagination, as much as we travel by the most rapid and most comfortable means of locomotion. Plant unknown species in the expanded lands, make the mountains join together.

Go down into the volcanoes and the destitutions, visible and invisible.

Do not believe in your uniqueness, or that your fable is the best one, or that your word is superior.

In this way, you will come to realize this, which is the strongest kind of knowledge: *that the place grows bigger in its irreducible centre, just as much as in its incalculable borders.*

2. *'Enough lamentations! Les us dare to move on. Let us come down the narrative into our present, and thrust it into the future! Let us explore the sufferings that are here now, in order to prevent those that will appear later.'*

I agree with this. Oh, yes! I agree. But let's be careful that our narrative does not get mixed up, perhaps, with this thread that has been spun for us. Let's not bite on this line. The world's narratives run round in circles, they don't follow the line, they have the impertinence of so many breaths, whose source is unsuspected. They rush down in all directions. Join in with them!

As for us, we were taught to tell: a story. To consent to History. To gild ourselves with the sparkle of its style, which we believe to be ours. We have been given the thread. But the folk tale does not tell a story, the folk tale does not count up our woes, it rushes forth from the hidden source of suffering and oppression, and it rejoices in unknown, perhaps obscure, kinds of happiness.

What you would call our narratives, they are perhaps like long breaths without beginning or end, where the times roll up on themselves. Diffracted times. Our narratives are long chants, treaties of joyful speech, and geographical maps, and joking prophecies, that don't care about verification.

Or perhaps, our narratives, those hastily sculptured pieces of bark, of mahogany, of ancient acoma, on which we recognize, just like on an identity card, the eyes the forehead the nose the mouth the chin of a black maroon.

3. Wandering is the very thing that allows us to fix ourselves. To leave these object lessons that we are so inclined to lecture on, to abdicate that tone of judgment with which we stifle our doubts – myself first of all – or our declamations, and to drift, finally.

Drift towards what? The fixity of the movement of the Whole-World. Those games of hopscotch, tragic, frenzied, meek or happy, that we play and whose horizons do not form the lines.

Wandering enables us to moor ourselves to that drift that does not get lost.

The thinking of wandering releases the imagination, projects us far from that imprisoning cave in which we were huddled, which is the hold or the rock of the so-called powerful uniqueness. We are greater, with all the variations of the world! With its absurdity, where nevertheless I imagine.

Then, looking all around us, we perceive only disaster. The impossible, the denial. But this sea that explodes, the Caribbean, and all the islands in the world, are Creole, unpredictable. And all the continents, whose coasts are immeasurable.

What is this voyage, which grasps its end in itself? Which stumbles into an ending?

The being and wandering have no end, change is their permanence! They continue.

Book 3

You ask why I am jumping about like this, going from polished sentences to all kinds of jumbles of words? And then, these acrobatics with time, Oriamé, Mycéa, Désira? I am imbued with landscapes, it's the only retreat I can have. Hidden beneath the river water, shining on the pavements of towns, asleep in the green of grass and tree, sparkling in the mirror of salt or sands, secretly tormented, those that enhance their skies, those that reveal the depths.

Time is one landscape and then another, as you walk on. You enter into the times, and there, you live more than you desire. The women are like the landscape. And if a woman changes and goes away, it's because for her too you are a landscape, and for her just as for you the countries call out. In this place where we live, they say it's cultural. A hybridity of men and women, of falling times, of horizons that move.

Many people however do not understand this. They are as cautious as an opossum. They try hard to evoke the world, they cannot. They cannot marry the landscapes together. They cannot choose all the women.

How would they know how to cry out? In this disorder and this energy, which story should one choose to tell? To take this diagonal and follow it to the end is an illusion. You still have the recitation of everything that trembles around you.

But, it seems, there is no longer even any need to imagine. You have at your disposal all these televisions and radios and newspapers. Which recite to you what they claim to be the novel of what is. You end up confusing one war with another. There is no peace. The instant has not joined up with duration, it has exploded in it. We must refuse this notion of the identical. We must attend to the depths.

1. Questioning the identical does not mean distracting from identity.

We observe how many old masters, now become master thinkers, delight in the speech of their flock, who used to be servants and at their beck and call, when this speech valiantly closes in on itself and resounds with supposedly primordial authenticity.

Argue, no less valiantly, that you are calculating not your being but your dwelling. Because you are leaving for faraway places. Don't be afraid that they will accuse you of working like an intellectual. They will do so in any case. It's because they are afraid that you are.

They share, the ex-master and the ex-slave, the belief that identity is a root, that the root is unique, and that whatever happens it must go one better.
Get ahead of all this. Go on!

Blow up this rock. Gather up the pieces and spread them out across the expanse of space.

Our identities relay each other, and so these hidden hierarchies, or those that surreptitiously maintain themselves under praise, fall away into futile claims. Do not agree to these manoeuvres of the identical.

Open up to the world the field of your identity.

2. Ah! We are afraid to go into the depths. The depths, for us, is the *mangle* and the mangrove. But we know that they are not the same.

The *mangle*: the water and the land at their edges, where we have lived. The land crabs, crabs of the depths. The fights of the wild cats and the vetiver trees. We were not a problem for the *mangle*. We loved roaming about in it (but at the risk of the thrashing that Marie-Euphémie had waiting for you when you got home, that was the price of the adventure). We took a lot from the *mangle*, without noticing. Dark, complicated, lost in the branchings of red roots, it began at the cemetery and gnawed at the coast with yellow water coming up against blue water, up to the mouth of the Rivière Salée. We saw the world in it: these possibilities that arose under our gaze.

The mangrove is this *mangle*, but once we have separated ourselves from it, because we have taken it over. The space is the same, the species also, but they are becoming rarer. Still that smell of rusty mud, of organic rubbish – still this throbbing of the water as it heats up. We crisscross the mangrove, we cover it with tracks and roads. We dig excavations into it, we fill it in. We try but in vain to reach its depths. It has retreated behind the mystery of its rubbish.

The mangrove is the *mangle* when it has been through our uncaring hands.

On the edge of the Mississippi river, facing the main square of the town, immediately in tune with the light and the noise as though it were a familiar place, we cut through the crowds of tourists, the carriages, the paintings on display, the distant, lost accents of the café music – we don't know if it's jazz or, more probably, old tunes that come from the past, the sonorous keys of memory.

The raucous chant of the *Natchez* announces its next departure. This riverboat, as traditional as it could be, takes tourists to the port of New Orleans. One would never have imagined that an organ sound could be so shrill. We had gone on this river tour once and had felt the boredom and the gentle emptiness. There is not much to see: the long convoys of barges, between the carcasses of the factories.

This river port has none of the strangeness of seaports. It is just as engaging. You come upon something strange in the air, that holds you there in suspense.

One question from the world runs through this air, flies in English, in French, in all the languages of the tourists: What are the results of the elections in South Africa?

✦ ✦ ✦

Waves and Backwashes

Waves

Everything bursts open, everything sounds and blows in the wind. Everything loses its way and goes down, only to rise again to this wind. It is nothing but assault, vertigo and, drifting, this time. Fields and hill and ravine, mountains and bays! A person who outdoes you in grand passion: a landscape. An imprisoned spring, a muddy delta. And then the cry and the word, in the moment and in duration. Everything to me is seasons and rhythms, that I push towards the single Season. Then I feel like the son and the stranger, together. In the language that I shout, my *langage* screeches in gusts. The gentle marshes fall silent. Stories unravel History. Everything to me is a wave, narrated! Everything to me is Béluse and is Longoué, that the wind slopes down.* The wave is a backwash, bewildered at constantly turning.

---

* Béluse and Longoué are the main characters of *Le Quatrième Siècle* (1964); Longoué reappears in subsequent novels.

There is an Italy also in the world of the moon. With its expanded regions, a North that brigades a South, mounted towns, painted landscapes, multiple languages ... I have suggested, it was in *L'Intention poétique*,* and following the Barbadian poet Edward Kamau Brathwaite, that for the Caribbean, 'unity is submarine'. A reference to transportation, the common place of the Caribbean peoples, and to the Africans thrown into the sea, weighed down with cannonballs, from the bridges of the slave ships. This 'buried' unity reveals and indicates that the relations between the components of Caribbean reality are not only rational and logical but above all subliminal, hidden, in constant transformation. To express this, that we share multilingually between us, it is *langage* that counts here, as it deflects the limits of the languages used.

---

* *L'Intention poétique*, a collection of Glissant's essays published in 1969.

The name Mathieu

These names that I inhabit are organized into archipelagos. They hesitate on the edge of some kind of density, that is perhaps a break, they find a way around any interpellation, which they move infinitely beyond, they wander and meet up, without my thinking about it.

The name Mathieu was given to me at my baptism (on St Matthew's day, 21st September), then abandoned in the customs and the bustle of childhood, taken up again by me (or by a demanding character, this Béluse) in imagination, and finished or started again by attaching itself to Mathieu Glissant. He is not aware – after Barbara and Pascal and Jérôme and Olivier, and in any case, in this year of 1996, he is only seven years old – of this long track along which his name has wandered.

I used to think that the name Glissant, probably handed out like most Antillean surnames, was the insolent reversal of the name of a settler, i.e. Senglis. Names in reverse mean something.

We foster in ourselves the instinct of illegitimacy, which here in the Antilles is a derivative of the extended African family, an instinct repressed by all kinds of official regulations, of which the advantages of Social Security are not the least effective. I have been called Glissant from about the age of nine, when my father 'recognized' me. Still today, primary school pupils miraculously re-encountered at Lamentin airport call me by the name that I had then, which there is no need to recall. These schoolfriends are becoming rarer and rarer and that name (which is my mother's) will no longer be applied to me – motor of an identity or beginning of a scattering – when these very old companions have gone, and myself with them. My mother is dead, hope carried her away. We must let the names that incline us to melancholy sleep inside us.

My local nickname will go away too, the private name reserved for friends, who had chosen it. It was 'Godbi', and we also had among us Apocal, Babsapin, Tikilic and Totol. Macaron, Chine, Sonderlo. The only one of this band whose name was not changed was Prisca: it was already surprising enough that a boy 'bore' this girl's name.

*

'Marie Celat laughed at our fondness for giving everything names, and if she accepted the disguises of individual names for which we showed such functional, precise, witty and irrational imagination (there are still today those among us, big fellows of over fifty, dignitaries of masonic lodges, elected politicians, poets disappeared elsewhere or solidly installed civil servants, who are indeed – in life and not in stories – called (for us) Apocal or Babesapin (with or without an "e") or Tikilik – Tikil, or Atikil or Atikilik, it's the same thing – or Godby (Godbi) or Totol, also known as Potolé, Prisca alone having escaped this practice of dispersion, for the reason that his official first name, feminine, fixed and invariable, was already enough of a nickname), she always claimed that we didn't call a possum a possum, or Le Lamentin, Le Lamentin' (*La case du commandeur*).

*

Such baroque nicknames, decided and agreed on by us, wove a pact, secret but part of the ordinary course of life. Neither the complicity nor the pact is ostentatious. It is like this all over the world, in the forgotten districts of big towns, tracks in the bush where people walk silently past each other, with just a slight gesture of the hand, villages crouching under their foliage, deep expanses of living desert. We would dive into the Lézarde, which is now nothing but a filthy line of yellow water streaked with plastic and rubbish ('The Lézarde like a trickle of mud alongside the landing strip', ibid), we would dance through the three days and three nights of carnival without stopping, we would breathlessly recite poems and inform ourselves as quickly as possible on the agricultural trade unions.

I have so many names within me, and so many countries, signified by my own. This is what Marie Celat taught me, as she roamed through our stories like an abandoned animal. Names wander within us, perhaps we also keep a load of them in reserve, one for the plain, one for the archipelago, one for the path or one for the desert. The dance of the names is in tune with the unfolding of the landscapes. One rushes down them or slowly follows their course. They accumulate lands and seas around them, and we never know if we are going to plunge into them to rest, or if we will perhaps join them up, wandering and open, with so many faraway beaches and rivers.

Filiation and legitimacy wove the fabric of continuous duration. They ensured that no discontinuity would intervene to break up the certainty or corrupt the belief. They established law on the territory. What caused tragedy were the moments in which they found themselves threatened, from within or from outside, either by the faults of their holders or the enterprises of usurpers. The epic poems and tragic songs relate all this. But what are we to do now? The territory of power is invisible and has no particular relationship to a land, a soil, a homestead. You can conquer a place without occupying it. This is what is called a market. The daughters are in Bamako while the mothers are in Rio. The fathers advise their children by email. The community's land is the ultimate wandering, where sometimes you take your house with you, like a wagon. Yet most people cling to this legitimacy, which they calculate still ensures their privilege. One might suppose for instance that one of the defects of democratic systems is that every person elected, on the strength of their acquired legitimacy, is as though fatally drawn into arrogance and self-importance, being unable to imagine that legitimacy can be temporary. States, religions, doctrines, nations, tribes, clans and families build their irreducible defences on such a certainty.

A reader writes to me that she has not read my work on Faulkner and his Yoknapatawpha county but that she is surprised at my interest in this backward little corner of Mississippi, or something like that. The work has no need to be defended and it would be ridiculous of me to do so. But I could reply that William Faulkner, through his questioning of the legitimacy of this closed place, by showing the perversions of its filiation, has opened it up to the dimension of the world.

The concept can be both open and closed, mysteriously.

Systematic thought abolishes that which in the concept is an opening up.

Trace thought confirms the concept as movement, and relates it: gives its narrative, places it in relation, sings its relativity.

The cypress trees gnawed by epiphytes, planted upright in the water of a Louisiana bayou; the giant ferns overhanging the sheer cliff of the Route de la Tracée in Martinique; the tide of vegetation, at Tikal in Guatemala, with, rising out of it, the galleons of the temple pyramids, with their flights of steps like so many oars waiting; the pathetic vigil of the palm trees, all over the hills of Santiago in Cuba; the opening of paths between the sugar cane plants, which imprison you in every direction; the hoarse fissures of buried ravines or great canyons open to the sky; the yellowing of the mangroves, bordering the emerald blue of the sea around the town of Pointe-à-Pitre in Guadeloupe; the bottomless barrels of the Guyanan rain that have always marked out the chaos of its forest; the overflowing rivers transporting earth, the Mississippi and the Amazon, and also the little streams drying up under their rocks; and the waterfalls transfixed in their infinite violence, El Salto del Angel, or tiny and secret below the rusts of time: the landscapes of the Americas are openness, immeasurability, a kind of irruption into spaces. The people's histories cling to them and carve out monuments, which the energy rising from the earth moves and changes infinitely.

Backwashes

We write in the presence of all the world's languages.

We share them without knowing them, we invite them to join the language that we use. Language is no longer the mirror of any Being. The languages are our landscapes, which the thrust of the day changes in us.

Opposed to standardization, to banalization, to linguistic oppression, to the reduction to universal pidgins. But knowing already that we will not save one language by letting the others perish.

For with every language that disappears a part of the human imagination is lost forever: a part of the forest, of the savannah or the crazy sidewalk.

The taste of tin plates, the flavour of food. The price of hunger.

The imagination radiates and reforms itself in the mingling of the Whole-World. The mingling of languages in turn is made comprehensible to us by the language that we use: our use of the language can no longer be monolingual.

If the French language had been offered to me or imposed on me (they tried, it's true) as the sole experience of its only traditional space, I would not have been able to use it. A language enriches itself by allowing us to trace our *langage* within it: the poetics of our relation to the words.

In the same way, a composite language such as Creole cannot be defended in the atavistic mode of uniqueness or closure. Closed uniqueness threatens the interweaving of languages today, and it is the weave of Diversity that supports them.

A *langage* is above all this: the crazy frequentation of the organic, of the specificity of a language and, at the same time, its sober opening onto Relation.

(*The backwash is repetition, which endlessly tears itself apart.*)

And of course, what we do not forget is forever in the future. We wait for a cyclone, year after year, in this drily archived procession of our catastrophes. We know that it will come, but from where, and when? On Guadeloupe again, on Dominica? The hurricanes swell in the depths of the Atlantic, they come spinning towards us, they pass between us, they pass over us. Who will be hit this time, oh mother Caribbean? Always the wind twisting, the forest in wild disarray, the volcano's voices spilling forth, the shaking that lays waste the black earth with its volleys of red earth. We draw on these extremes and we reinforce ourselves with this violence, without knowing it. This danger preserves us from the certainties that would limit us.

The Time of the Other

Measure is seen as responding to a search for depth: one of the ways taken in the quest for the essence of things, a regulation of the pursuit of the True. The writing of the European languages, and in particular of French, complies with this: an architecture in which, as though in the nave of a sacred site, our singing rises up towards a presence that remains unattainable. This kind of measure, paradoxically, is wholly a sequencing, a metrics. The arrangement of a rhythm, which is a pre-existing rule, creates and expresses the mystery, or the depth. Metrics and prosody are protective obstacles.

Measure is also seen as the echo of the human breath. No longer the search for depth but the inspiration of the spatial expanse. This kind of measure enables us to drift through the fullness (or the surface) of the world, bringing it back to our own place.

At the beginning of 'universal' Western time

The European Middle Ages fascinate us, and not just because the West for a long time imposed its models on almost everyone else, until the movement of the histories of peoples plunged us into other modes of knowledge. We find there both the dawn and the night, and that indistinct moment when all things seem to hesitate on the edge of their singularity, both drawn to it and troubled by it.

Midnight-midday. An age of bursting forth that is also a beginning of time. Conducive to both lucid wakefulness and tormented sleep.

One is tempted to link it to other periods, to what we think we know, albeit only slightly, about the different cultural zones of the world. Ages that are said to be dark, periods of renaissance, eras of classicism, times of transformation and revolution: we are inclined to find elsewhere this movement of European histories, which has had implications for the whole world. We believe that we are approaching both a mystery and its resolution. Influenced by the formidable powers of persuasion of the Western linear time that was conceived in this half-shadow, a time that we tend to consider a definitive result, we find ourselves almost adopting, in our exploration of this period, the attitudes and formulations of the sorcerer's apprentice – convinced that we can easily gain an overview of it and that, as with modern chaos theory, we grasp its principal themes. Illusions that are emphasized by our innocently pedantic exposition of our knowledge, which will certainly irritate specialists in the subject.

The apparent disorder that seems to us to overwhelm these European Middle Ages is the main reason why we have linked it to our time (our times). Peoples and people today, who have had the privilege of reflecting on the passage of times and on their 'reunion' in a planet-wide intermingling, perhaps feel that the bursting open of our world will be followed by another beginning. The mystery, and its resolution. Such a hope, teleological in its inspiration, has made the European Middle Ages a precious object of study.

By its multiplicity first of all. For example, the multiple centres or cultural focus points, of which the main ones are: the Flemish or Nordic centre, where the tendency to mystical thought is dominant; the Celtic centre, in both islands and the mainland, where the ancient Gods and ancient powers unceasingly disappear and are reborn; the Languedoc centre, creator of fruitful heresies; the Provençal and Italo-Lombardian centre, which glories in allegory and brings the joyfulness of the representation of the world; the Norman centre and the Île-de-France, which extends (and vice versa) into England and where there is very soon a strengthening of these attempts at synthesis and resolution that will end up as sumptuous autocentrisms.

These centres influence each other or fight each other, and quickly discover the secret of meetings with other sites of thought, classical Greek or Roman, Hebrew or Arabic, and consent to learn from them. Diversity does not at first lapse into self-sufficiency, and the cultures do not isolate themselves in sectarian complacency, at least not yet. It is at the *turning point* of the Middle Ages, once the muffled conflict that underlies this period (between wandering thought and systematic thought) has been resolved, that this whole constellation will keel over into the Unique, accompanying on the one hand the constitution of nations that are antagonistic towards each other but constituted on the same rationalizing model, and on the other hand the introduction of a universality of belief that will very soon become a belief in the universal.

There are two constant factors that work to crystallize, in the melting pot of this period, the whirlpool of opposites that, attracting and repelling each other, will 'produce the universal'. The influence of the Middle East, less noticeable and immediate than that of Greece and Byzantium, for what concerns the science of Being. And technical needs, which are behind the huge wave of practical inventions in the Middle Ages and prefigure, with the first attempts at experimentation (such as those of Roger Bacon) a science of the world.

*

The melting pot, the universality of belief, the force that impels this play of opposites, is Faith. So that Gustave Cohen* can sum it up like this:

'Everything here [i.e. in the Middle Ages] is seen from the angle of the Universal, Infinity and God, so that every object of perception appears as a reflection of the Cosmos, and this is the principle greatness of this time.'

Can it be proved that this lack of differentiation between the Universal, God, the Infinite and the Cosmos is admissible? God 'represents', for the Middle Ages, the supreme answer to the impossibilities or the unknowns of the Infinite and the Cosmos. In the eleventh century St Anselm

---

* A French medievalist, 1879–1958.

pronounces the '*Credo ut intelligam*', 'I believe in order to understand', which is not far off from 'I believe because I understand', and which increases the rationality of the '*nisi credideritis non intellegetis*' of Isaiah, taken up again the in the ninth century by John Scotus, otherwise known as Eriugena.

But St Anselm's formula is the best example of the opposition between this attempt at Christian rationality, which culminates in the Summa of Albert the Great and of Thomas Aquinas, and the temptations of the thought of the Infinite and the Cosmos, which during the same period follows more obscure paths, indirect and usually forbidden. Although unbelievers are rare, the mode of accession to knowledge through faith remains questionable. The luminous mysteries of the intelligible may for example seem less attractive than the ineffable experience of mystical intuition. Or the rough stature of thought that refuses to 'understand' the unknowable in a system of reassuring transparency and prefers to confront the impossible. There are no atheists, only heretics.

Mystical experiences and approaches based on knowledge are engaged in the same quest for *a total knowledge*, and one can say that in this sense Ramon Llul (who wrote *The Book of the Friend and the Beloved*) does not contradict Thomas Aquinas. But what is at stake is crucial, regarding the mode and soon the nature of knowledge, and will influence and orientate this set of cultures that will go on to dominate the world. Particular or ecstatic invention will give way to rationalizing bodies of thought and then to the absolute generalization of systematic thought, Descartes or Leibniz. *What the West will export to the rest of the world, will impose on the world, will not be its heresies but its systems of thought, its systematic thought.* English empiricism, Locke or Hume, despite its determination to refute the generalizations of thought, will nevertheless constitute a generalization of a different kind, a self-sufficient system, which will itself contribute to repressing the ardent and tumultuous mêlée of the Middle Ages.

Two stances, two opposing orders, two extremes in the search for knowledge: the Middle Ages will be the scene of their opposition and, when systematic thought has won, the Universal, first Christian and then rationalist, will take over as the specific achievement of the West, even after the latter has prepared what Nietzsche called the death of God.

The unique feature of this period is to have been the theatre for such a long quarrel, to have lived through the anxiety of such a decisive dispute, of a suspense that plunged the being into Gehenna, and to have first of all tried to put forward a response that was flamboyant, solar and lunar, totalizing: that of the heresies, which was opposed to generalization, to Summa, to systematic thought.

*

The feverish, breathless quality of medieval faith, and also its inhuman enormities, accompany this enterprise whose changes bring together the demand for belief and the demand for obedience, heroic heresy and the Inquisition, tolerance and the Crusades, Jewish teachings and the pogroms, Arabic medicine or philosophy and anti-Saracen racism, Thomist pre-rationalism and sombre Cathar penitence, the feudal turbulences and the search for monarchist order, the supporters of the pope and the servants of the emperor, scholastic knowledge and nocturnal knowledge.

Wild and shadowy, or mystical and feverish, or pre-rationalist and dreamily lucid, according to the common place that we have made of it and given it, medieval faith remains the detour whereby these cultures, through massacres and violent deaths, tried to bring about the progress, or simply the salvation, of the individual, so that he could accede to the dignity of the human person. This is why, in this faith, a special status was accorded to Jesus Christ, who became man, and to Our Lady, who is his mother without sin. Individuation is a primary mystery, and the individuation of Christ opened up the way to its becoming general. It alone could do that. If the whole of man, flesh, soul and spirit, is in Christ, then the universal can take off. Still today, Western cultures hold together the generality of the Universal and the dignity of the human individual, in spite of all the brutalities, oppressions and exploitations that their societies have inflicted on the world.

After that of the Incarnation, the other question that tormented for example the thinkers of the Carolingian Middle Ages, Alcuin or Eriugena, revolved around the impossibilities of the Resurrection and was formulated as follows: how does the soul separate itself from the body? – in other words: how do bodies 'become' spirit?

Let us not forget that in the seventeenth century Descartes was still proposing to solve the problems of the relation between body and mind only by the hypothesis of animal spirits.

These same torments, in so many different forms, overwhelm medieval thinking. How could animality, which was responsible for the fall, be transcended in Love – in courtly love? How might the individual contain or resume in his imperfections the absolute dimension of the person? This will later be Pascal's question. Should the diverging temporal authorities not submit to a single spiritual authority? How could matter, in its gross disruptions, lead to the pure receptacle of the philosophers' stone? And, finally – this will become the question of Montaigne's time – how could diversity raise itself up into universality? But we know that Montaigne, in his time, will mistrust universal resolution.

A dialectical torment, and one that affects all levels, from the metaphysical to the technical. Transmute the disparate weights of marble and stone into the convergent momentum and daring of the arch, and you will have cathedrals.

Call for the single Word in the silence, which is the annulment of the diversity of voices, and it will be the cloister.

A number of technical inventions are thus motivated or secretly impelled by this pressure to support the Unique, even if this is not yet scientific.

The clock challenges the disparities of solar and lunar time, and calls for the universal of an absolute time. Polyphony is the perfect unitary resolution of diversities of sound and voice, insufficient to themselves in their specificity.

The space of the world, the time of the world, the sound of the world will be transcended in intelligible perfection.

The mystical experiences and the rationalizing summae are identical in nature. The latter, the Summae, hold out the promise of access to a soothing totality, where mysteries are accepted with all the will of the person. It is not surprising that the principles of Aristotle's *Organon* should at first have led in this direction. The former, the mystical experiences, do not plunge the individual into the closed depths of the singular but into the ecstasy of a super-knowledge of the Whole. The heresies alone preserve, powerfully, the voice of specificities, the piling up of irreducible diversities, and finally the determination not to try to 'understand' the unknown, just in order to then generalize it into formulae and systems. But they will be swept away.

We admire the poet Marcabru's claim that the people of France accept the 'afar Deu': the 'thing of God', perhaps the Thing-God, or perhaps the affair of God, or the Affair-God.

The multiple meaning of such an expression, of such an image, suggests that it has to do with a sacred expedient, a sacred detour, in order to 'understand' oneself as essence and project. God is the all-powerful generalizer, and so the vector of a human, an all too human power, which will soon engender the thinking of the Universal.

Therefore the question that I would ask about the European Middle Ages is not that of the opposition of Reason and Faith, since both of these will endeavour to reach this Universal, and will succeed, that is to say not in 'realizing' it, but in imposing it. Rather, my question is the following: why, in this search for knowledge, have the paths of the non-generalizing, of the esoteric for instance (which is always marked with the sign of the ambiguous and the unpredictable), and the mystical, in any case of heresy, gradually given way to the striving towards totalitarian generalization? Why has the rationality of the Universal become the precious and semi-exclusive claim of this collection of cultures that has been called the West?

In my mind I hurtle down spaces and times, the rivers of China and their smooth silence, which extend into archipelagos and overflow into the lands, each time engulfing many thousands of men and women and children in their ritual floods, the calendars of Heaven that preside over the destinies of Empire, and the hiding places in the bush and the Chain of Ancestors of the African countries, the savannahs pulsing beneath their grasses laid low by heat and the stories of the *griots* imbued with a wisdom that grows into a shade-giving tree, the delicate details of the Indian mythologies with their green marble and their gymnastic couplings, the temples pillaged in the peaks of the Andes and the oblique words of the Amerindian Myths, the chronicles of the hundred kingdoms of feudal times in Japan, the shortened proverbs of the Madagascan and Oceanic and Caribbean countries and the archipelago of the Indian Ocean, the splendours of the desert and of pre-Islamic rhetoric, and the drapes of their women poets, half slaves and half goddesses, the stiff and gentle baroque of Creole languages, and so many flowery anthologies declaimed in so many islands, and the stone roots lifting up gods who can see everything, in the flooded gorges of the Indo-Chinese peninsula, and the swell and the backwash of all the seas ploughed in circles by their peoples (not that deadly projection towards new lands to be conquered), I cross the heights of yet more deserts, deserts that are always around and that are in fact truly universal, and the silences of the Sierras, I quake with the earthquakes and the eye of the hurricane is watching me, and so many wars have ravaged everywhere that there are no longer any dreams where one could gather oneself, and so many unfathomable epidemics have eaten up the thought of the world like a rotten overripe fruit, I travel the twelve routes of Egypt's *Book of the Dead*, and the enormous flatness of towns crackles on the edge of the Archipelagos, carrying its mangroves of poverty and sudden sounds, I admire everywhere so many inventions, techniques woven into the humble artisanal energy of every day, I shout so many poems and I try to decipher so many depths, but nowhere in the little that I know and in nothing of what I imagine of this world, do I come across the ardent stigmata of that rigid will that leads to the Universal, of which the Middle Ages were the battleground, the arena and the painful and triumphant resolution.

*

There is no point in stating that Reason was born with the Greeks and that the medieval period gradually rediscovered and then extended its principles, which will be perfected in the following centuries. Reason could have developed on the margins of generalization. Of all the civilizations, that of the West is the only one to have experienced this drive towards generalized expansion, conquest, knowledge and faith, all inextricable, which required the Universal as a guarantee of its legitimacy. The European Middle Ages lived through the tumultuous struggle between the Diverse and its constraining opposite, the struggle of particular beliefs and universal belief, and, fighting against itself, let go (this is its suffering and its victory, which is why it is fascinating) of the weave of illegitimate diversity, the daring of fragmented knowledge, not total and systematic but so totalizing and wandering.

In times when writing conferred privilege on certain individuals, chosen ones in chosen peoples, the writer was free to distance himself from the world or the idea of the world. But it is true that today the very substance of his work is expanded by that which constitutes it: the entanglement of human communities and things and vegetation, the rocks and the clouds of our universe. In solidarity and in solitude, he engages in the debate, from the depths of his work. That is why in so many places people want to silence writers. Banning their words (for all the sworn opponents of the existent) is a way of deepening the shadow in the very darkness in this entanglement.

End-of-Century Rhetorics

The division of Western linear time into centuries has a specific relevance. It becomes part of the unconscious of the peoples of this region of our earth, it has entered into our common sensibility, it has imposed itself everywhere, it has marked a rhythm.

It is part of the very principle of History. And even capable of swallowing up, digesting perhaps, the intrusions of the histories of peoples, of forcibly inscribing them into its linearity. There are only advantages in accepting this linearity of time, whether it is determined on the basis of the birth of Jesus Christ or the start of the Hegira or the first Jewish Passover.

But at the same time, to refuse or question this division into centuries is already to challenge, perhaps without knowing or really wanting to, the universalizing generalization of Judeo-Christian time. A role that has fallen to diversifying thoughts, mad poets and heretical relativists.

In fact, if there is a feeling of unreality in contemporary Europe, just as it tries to create itself, this is not because of the well-known torments that one feels at the end of a century, but because of the enormous multiplicity in which History is now going astray, and the pain caused by the lack of power or control over this History, felt by those who had conceived it as an origin projecting itself towards an end.

This was at stake in the systems of relation, so baroque and so precious, decided not so long ago by European thinkers, between a diachrony posed as a neutral movement (a History without flesh) and a synchrony placed there as a time without object. These systems, which engendered rhetorics, did not bear witness to a millennial fear, but, very subtly, to a consciousness of the new multiplicity of the world and the nostalgia of no longer being able to govern it, of no longer making History. These rhetorics are the ingenious lasso or the rope that Western thought (at its most alert) has put around the neck of History.

That is what they do. Relativize History, but without being willing to accept the histories of peoples.

If the end of the century (and the end of this century) seems significant, it is because at the same time, so to speak, it has kept its function as the pendulum of linear time, but, already taken unawares by the multiplicity of times and histories that have risen up from the depths of the world and are finally joining together, its significance is no longer so absolute.

*

'We would also sing of what people said was the approaching end of the century; and although we didn't know which century or in relation to what, we could feel that it referred to whole heap of time, an incalculable number of harvests: this end surrounded us with a sadness full of strange bursts of joy, of excitement at something beyond the end. We sang:

The end of the century is the end of poverty
The century and us we are undressed
A century is dead and buried
The Negro is a century and has lost his true self.

That was our way of marking the passage of time. Adoline too seemed to be moving towards her end. She was more than a century that rolls into decadence, she was a century full of its own fallen greenery. She was falling, like the greenery of the country attacked by burnings and axes. The country was growing less dark, like a shack whose walls of planks let in bursts of the flower of sunlight at midday. We were going from the civilization of the forest to the civilization of the savannah: at least that is what we would have said if we had owned a little more land in a little more time ...'

(*La case du commandeur*)

*

Having thus considered that, in these countries where the gulfs of time and the vertigo of collective memory give birth to so many cries, the rhythm of our words perhaps follows the lines of a secret disorder, I have chosen to summarize here some aspects of our oral rhetorics, in the provocative form of the memorandum, the ultimate in writing.

Rhetorics of Orality, or Not

(Summary)

Introduction: What Orality Is Not

It is difficult to develop or explore a rhetoric, an art of speech and the spoken word, when writing is today tempted, tormented, with the evident but unclear passions of the oral.

It is not a question of a simple transition from the written to the oral, as is sometimes said. Nor of knowing if one should replace texts conceived for contemplation or meditation (for the 'inner voice', in some sense) with texts of a different kind, constructed for declamation and hearing.

When we envisage the histories of human communities, we see that they all involved the relay between the oral and the written, that is to say, where writing appeared first as progress, then as transcendence. The foundational books stand tall like monuments on the frontiers of these countries where voices were gradually fixed onto concrete objects, tablets, rocks, monuments and parchments. The *Iliad* and the *Old Testament* for example bring together the tracks of the earlier oral traditions and fix them, obliging the singer to repeat them in this fixed form.

It is a question of speculating, tentatively, as to whether this transcendence in which writing had been established will now be challenged. The languages and practices of orality have reappeared in the panorama of literatures, they have begun to influence its sensibility with flamboyant energy and presence. We must think, passionately, not how to manage this transition, now from the written to the oral, but how to encourage a renewed poetics where the oral would remain a force in the written, and vice versa, and where the exchange between the spoken languages of the world would burn brightly.

Such new kinds of poetics are not to be confused with the old dramatic art or the tricks of 'spoken' writing. Writing in drama and the 'spoken language' of novels are literary procedures, that question neither the nature nor the status of the written.

Moreover we must not accept the media effects of the audiovisual and the written press. These effects use techniques – news flash, script, scenario, short report – that claim to represent reality in an abbreviated form that is almost always oversimplified. There is no orality there. There is nothing but brief pieces of writing, arranged for recording or filming. Writing is never fruitfully brief except when it inhabits or borders on silence, but without disappearing. From the point of view of a rhetoric of writing, the brevity of the audiovisual is always idle chatter.

It is also a way of playing tricks with the real: they try to capture what is essential in reality and claim to describe it in its totality, whereas in fact they have carefully chosen from it, isolated or readjusted something that they will illustrate and present as permanent or definitive. If 'representation' of the real is the law of the audiovisual, the mimesis here is deceptive: it acts in a present time that is always fleeting. This helps us to understand that the imitation of the real, one of the foundations of writing in Western cultures, has to be re-examined.

And if the 'duplication' of the real is at the basis of the world of computers, we must know or suspect all that such a redoubling opens up in variations, beyond an elementary cloning that would have been without echoes.

Orality, this passion of the peoples who in the twentieth century have emerged into the visibility of the world, and in so far as it enters writing, manifests itself first through the fruitful quarrels it introduces there, multiplicity, circularity, repetitions, accumulation and irreligion. Relation in fact.

It escapes from the systems of traditional rhetorics which always supported a linearity or a unity of time and language.

1. *Multiplicity, Circularity*

The histories (that have emerged) of the peoples that are now visible dissipate the linear harmony of time

It is not certain that in the world-totality the temporal linearity consecrated by the expansion of Western cultures can be maintained as a universal *regulatio*. At least on the level of the imagination.

In these circumstances, neither the 'century' nor its end any longer have any normative value

One can imagine contemporary peoples who live different times and who continue to be in action and reaction with other presences in the Chaos-World. And who thereby express 'ends' that diverge from the temporal norm accepted by everyone.

In this sense, and for our time, each year, each day, each minute can be a century or the end of a century. And also each individual. This is summed up in the Antillean proverb that says: 'A Negro is a century'. Not so much that he endures, or that his resentment is patient, as that he is impenetrable and one cannot see through him.

The traditional rhetorics continue to be monolingual and unilateral

They cannot conceive of the diffractions of our times, or the distances and vertiginous attractions between all given languages. They can conceive of themselves only in the use of a single language, which has delimited its periods in the linearity that we have said (before and after Jesus Christ). But, oh Rabelais, oh Joyce, oh Pound, oh playful entanglements.

The non-hierarchical multiplicity of languages leads irreversibly to new langages

The phenomena of creolization at work in our world concern not only the diversity of times experienced by communities which may or may not be in contact, but also the interchange of the written and spoken languages. Beyond these languages, the imagination (or imaginations) of human communities could inspire *langages*, or archipelagos of *langages*, which would be the equivalent of the infinite variation of our relations. Language is the ever shattered crucible of my unity. *Langage* would be the open field of my Relation.

Transrhetorics, whose usages are not yet known to us.

End of Century or End of History?

Will the twentieth century really come to its end? Can we not rather consider that what is endlessly ending for us is History, or rather the philosophies of History, which have constructed normative linearity and at the same time defined their own exclusive finality in the torment of human times?

Transhistory is spreading.

II. Accumulation and Irreligion

Orality Outside Transcendence
The transcendence of writing compared to orality, particularly in Western cultures, is based on the ambiguity of the term Word, where one cannot actually distinguish if it designates only the spoken word of God or also the form of his written Law. Every case of the transcendence of writing results from an absolute of Revelation. Of a primary Dictation, just as determining as a Genesis.

Works of orality, especially when it is composite and not atavistic, are woven in Relation. The Sacred for us perhaps comes from this Relation, no longer from a Revelation or a Law.

Poetics of the Oral-Written
These do not constitute systems of rhetoric.
One could list their themes, without having to order them:
A poetics of duration, which does not 'itemize' the different times.
Piling up and accumulation, which take the word out of its linearity.
Return and repetition, which do not cheat the signified.
Rhythms of assonance, which weave the memory of our surroundings.
The obscure, which is the echo of the Chaos-World.

III. Poetics of Relation, Poetics of Chaos

Rhetoric and Identity.
Let us repeat that what we have discussed here is linked to the conception that everyone has of his or her identity.

The Being-Root is exclusive, it does not enter into the infinite and unpredictable variations of the Chaos-World, where only being-as-Relation is active.

The traditional rhetorics could be seen as the glorious effort of the Being-Root to confirm itself as Being.

Relation, Unpredictable, Cannot Conceive of Rhetoric.
Where the written associated itself with transcendence and tried to illustrate Being, the oral-written-oral multiplies openness and traces its

path in the flaming impromptu of the world, which is the only form of its permanence.

The Chaos-World, Unpredictable, Multiplies Rhetorics
Also, a *system* can be conceived in this context only if it 'comprehends' all envisageable rhetorics, and also all the possibilities of a non-universalizing trans-rhetoric.

The words of the Chaos-World do not presuppose any normative generalization.

The burning light projects limitlessly.

And there, quite suddenly, the crazy arum lilies, the red gingers, sculpted scentless flowers, steal from the Balata forest* its writing: the muffled propagation of its sparkling incense.

---

* 'Le Jardin de Balata' is a well-known, partially 'wild', garden in Martinique.

For baroque art, knowledge grows through extension, accumulation, proliferation and repetition, and not above all through depths and dazzling revelation. Baroque is usually of the order (or the disorder) of orality. In the Americas it meets up with the ever-renewed beauty of hybridities and creolizations, where the angels are Indian, the Virgin black, the cathedrals like vegetation in stone, and this echoes the words of the story-teller which also spread through the tropical night, accumulate and repeat. The story-teller is Creole or Quechua, Navajo or Cajun. In the Americas, the baroque is naturalized.

Writing

To write is to say: the world.

The world as totality, which is so dangerously close to the totalitarian. No science can give us a truly global opinion of it, can enable us to appreciate its extraordinary hybridity, or can reveal to us how much living in it changes us. Writing, which leads us to unpredictable intuitions, allows us to discover the hidden constants of the world's diversity, and we are happy to feel how these invariables also speak to us.

This saying of writing, which thus brings us closer to such a knowledge, also means that we can feel why it is the world as totality, and not an exclusive, chosen or privileged part of the world, that transports us.

We discover that the place that we live in, that we speak from, can no longer be separated from this mass of energy that calls to us in the distance. We can no longer grasp its movement, its infinite variations, its sufferings and its pleasures, unless we relate it to that which moves so totally for us, in the totality of the world. The 'exclusive part' that would be our place, we cannot express its exclusivity if we make of it an exclusion. We would then have a totality that really did border on totalitarianism. But, instead of that, we establish Relation.

And not by an abstraction, an idealization of everything, that would have led us to see in our particular place a sort of reflection of a beneficial, profitable universal. We have renounced that as well. The claim that one has abstracted a universal from a particular no longer excites us. It is the actual substance of each of the places, their minute or infinite detail and the thrilling sum of their particularities, that is to be placed in complicity with those of all places. To write is to summon up the savour of the world.

The idea of the world is no longer sufficient. A literature based on the idea of the world may be skilful, ingenious, giving the impression of having 'seen' the totality (this is for example what in English is called 'World Literature'), but it will pontificate in non-places and be nothing but an ingenious destructuring and a hasty recomposition. The idea of the world takes advantage of the imagination of the world, the intertwined poetics that allow me to sense how my place joins up with others, how without moving it ventures elsewhere, and how it carries me along in this immobile movement.

*

Writing is saying, literally.

The brilliance of the spoken word is the manifesto of all those peoples who are suddenly clamouring to sing their languages, before they perhaps disappear, worn out and erased by the international pidgins. The adventure is beginning, for all these oral languages, that up to now have been despised and dominated. Standardizations, transcriptions, with their traps that must be avoided; but also, the inscription of these languages within a social formation that perhaps tends, or is forced, to use what is called a major language of communication, a dominant language. The diversity of the world needs the languages of the world.

The brilliance of the oral literatures has thus come, not of course to replace the written text, but to change its structure. Writing really is saying: opening up to the world without dispersing or diluting oneself in it, and without being afraid to use in writing those powers of orality that are so much in accordance with the diversity of all things: repetition, accumulation, circularity, the spiralling cry, the breaks in the voice.

In this new state of literature, the ancient and very fruitful division into literary genres is perhaps no longer compulsory. What is a novel and what is a poem? We no longer believe that narrative is the natural form of writing. The story that one tells and controls used to be inherent to the History that one makes and governs. The latter was the guarantee of the former, for the peoples of the West, and the former was the legitimate celebration of the latter. There is still some prestige attaching to this solidarity in the popularity of fashionable novels, in Europe and the Americas. But we are drawn to different forms. The explosion of the world-totality and the rushing towards audiovisual or computerized techniques have opened the field to an infinite variety of possible genres, of which we have as yet no idea. Meanwhile, the poetics of the world are gaily mixing up genres, thus reinventing them. This means that our collective memory is prophetic: at the same time as it assembles the given of the world, it tries to remove from it the elements that encouraged hierarchy, the scale of values, a falsely transparent universal. We know today that there is no model that works.

*

The poet, beyond the language that he uses, but mysteriously within that very language, on the level of the language and in its margin, is a builder of *langage*. The clever but mechanical game-playing of languages may soon appear outdated, but not the work that churns away at the base of *langage*. The poet attempts to rhizomatically connect his place to the totality, to diffuse the totality into his place: permanence in the moment and vice versa, the elsewhere in the here and vice versa. That is the small amount of divination that he claims for himself, faced with the derelictions of our reality. He does not play the game of the universal, which would not be a way of establishing Relation. He always supposes, from the first word of his poem: 'I speak to you in your language, and I hear you in my *langage*'.

Towns, big villages of nothing! Real places of the All! Have you lost your *Xamaniers** and your *arapes*? The end of the evening, what is left of its cloud, has run away over the acacias. Now it is late, you have no more paths left to plough. Your *daciers* fight with your assembled Majors. Your smoke becomes visible in the carobs as they grow cold. The storm has gone up into the hills of your *salènes*. You mix up the words and the languages and the echoes with the solidified mud of the *huques*. You create new ones. It's a *langage*, which infiltrates the grease of your roads, we hear it, we speak it. You stay there, heavy with the weight of so many breaths. Without even seeing that we grind your spelt flour on your rose bushes.

---

* The italicized words in this passage are words that Glissant has invented, as he explains in a note at the end of the book.

❖ ❖ ❖

What Was Us, What Is Us

... The flames of the wild lilies, the bright thickets of birds of paradise, the sleepy reddish houses looking out over marshes scattered with ginger torches, and all the laughs and sorrows that the world-totality amasses in a single favela, then the sands – Brazil – cascading down between the walls of snaking rivers, and the cries of choirs from Africa mixing with the Indian flute, from where the bossa nova will soon emerge, and the yapping of the factories coming to lick the mosaics of the pavements, all these familiar images that accumulate immeasurably, and the Amazonian peacocks that engulf the families of the forest in the shadow of their spreading tails, and the rough smell of the coconuts and the bitter oranges ...

Folding and Unfolding

> *And for all your life you will descend this staircase*
> Michel Leiris, *Aurora*

Michel Leiris's meticulous observation does not betoken a fragmented vision of the real, but leads him to an accumulation of details (or of episodes) that ultimately makes up a weave. This meticulousness responded to an aspect of his character. Closed in on himself, cautious and perhaps suffering from shyness, he made an effort to pay genuine and serious attention to others and to the world. He read the real with a frenzied or delighted determination, because he distrusted his natural absent-mindedness or his egotism. And what he thus read, he balanced with his understanding of himself, seeking a correlation between self and other. It all came back to the individual Michel Leiris, but through modesty, through a fear of creating or seemingly wanting to impose established or definitive truths.

The real is a totality which is forever weaving itself. Michel Leiris's passion will be to decipher this weave and to give it a poetic equivalent, but not for just anyone: in every corner where he had a chance of coming upon himself, everywhere he would find himself implicated in the Other, every word that would activate this relationship.

*

In one of his first books, *Aurora* ('I was not yet thirty when I wrote *Aurora* ...'), Leiris shows this kind of to-and-fro, emphasizing for example this:

> The death of the world equates with the death of myself, no adherent of a cult of unhappiness will make me reject this equation, the sole truth that dares claim my agreement, even though contradictorily I occasionally sense everything that the word HE may hold for me in vague punishments and monstrous threats (p. 40)*

---

* The quotations all relate to the re-edition of *Aurora* in the collection *L'Imaginaire* (Gallimard, 1977).

The real is a body of meanderings and life throbs in every corner of it. The real and life make up the folding. Considering them together comes down to building a rhetoric, by a slow work of unfolding that aims to enlighten rather than to convince, to persuade oneself rather than confusing the reader – the mute confident – with an excess of reasons.

The same approach governs observation, or vision, in *L'Afrique fantôme*. Although the book's title constitutes a presupposition (it is Leiris who is the 'fantom', searching in vain for himself), the material that fills it does not consist of theoretical suppositions. A rigorous observer, and one who imposes on himself the most formal objectivity in his notation, Leiris nevertheless puts into practice, on occasion, this sustained relationship between subjectivity and the real that will be the basis for his life's work.

Scrupulous objectivity, which is the rule of the profession. Subjectivity, which enters into ethnographic thinking. The relation to the other (or at least the anxious search for it), which is an implication of modesty. The determination not to conclude with generalizing theory.

We might add suspense, that way of leaving his conclusions until later but picking up yesterday's detail or episode, and imperceptibly adding to it. The weave. Suspense will be one of the features of the art of Leiris's writing prose, a suspense that is not frivolous but is repeated as part of the spatial expanse and the duration of the writing.

This was the period when a conception of 'pure' ethnology was being elaborated: the attempt to discover, based on the model of societies that were also assumed to be pure, or at least less complex (which was in itself a strange prejudice), the elementary structures or dynamics of any given society. The claims of this dominant ethnology were once again based on objectivity, but in the sense of a will or belief that one can contain the essence of a social or cultural fact in the mesh of the descriptions; on distancing, whereby one hoped to guarantee objectivity; on definition, which presupposes that the observed phenomenon has been completely understood, in addition to its exemplarity. Leiris does not subscribe to this temptation of the generalizing universal.

*

His most significant work in this instance is *Contacts de civilisations en Guadeloupe et en Martinique*, a book which is not much discussed, for good reason: how does one assess this punctilious accumulation of facts, which does not lead on to foundational theories but leaves in its raw state the real that it has uncovered, content just to weave in its mass? Leiris as ethnographer, in the pragmatic, humble way that typified his approach to things and people, here accepts the analytical schemas common to anthropology and sociology: the study of social classes and levels of *langage*, the examination of historical 'formations'. But one soon realizes that, faced with the complex reality of the French-speaking Antilles, composite Creole societies, what retains his attention is not the subject matter (to be discovered or 'understood') of this reality, but first and foremost the complexity itself as subject matter. We are fully within an ethnology of Relation, an ethnography of the relation to the Other.

To study contacts between cultures means one has already decided that there is no lesson to be learnt from them, since the nature of such contacts is to be fluid and unexpected. We would also say (linking the quality of this observed reality, or of the account that is given of it, to the observer himself), that Leiris did not intend to draw any conclusion from his self-analysis, other than to envisage day after day that other conclusion, which is also a suspension, and which he was obsessed by: the moment of his death. Not death as possible fear (such as Montaigne tried to remedy in advance) but death as a mystery or scandal ending another scandal or mystery, that of life. 'Night and day death hung over me like a dismal threat' (p. 84).

*

If the observation of the real and the confession of oneself do not aim to uncover the basic reality of things, what is the point of them? As far as ethnography is concerned, it is a question of describing honestly in order to better establish a connection, to better found the exchange. As for the confession, or let's say the confidence, we are so enmeshed in the tissue of the work that we do not notice one of its obvious features: that Leiris does not really inform us of the elements of his life – the women he has desired, the resentments he has experienced, the lacks he suffers – except in a secondary and in some sense illusory fashion.

Confession in his case has nothing in common with how we understand it in Rousseau for example: an exaltation of the ego, the justification of an existence and a way of thinking. Nor does it correspond to the search for an indubitable truth.

It is this same pitiless demand for truth (for veracity) in detail that is imposed here (for confession) and there (for the practice of ethnography). The attention with which Leiris observes the world is governed by the all-powerful nature of this veracity, more difficult to achieve in the case of confession. For Leiris, the most demanding element is the eye. Not only the eye that sees in the present, but also the eye of memory, which hears words coming from so far away, tormenting expressions, tunes, proverbs, common places.

Thus we discover the principle, which we had struggled to seize, of confession for Leiris: to contribute to the weave of a rhetoric that is alone capable (establishing a relationship between living and saying) of providing an excuse for the scandal of the human condition, in other words, of *his* condition. 'We do not arrive on earth with impunity and any kind of escape is impossible' (p. 58).

*

The demand for truth comes before everything else. If the elements that are linked together in the poetics, the words, the expressions, these proverbs, these tunes, from which the author 'starts', or the events that he 'uses', had first been deformed or fantasized by him, then the link between the condition and its expression, the weave of the real and the weave of saying, would have been broken. And if one merged together these two dimensions, of living and saying, without bringing to them the ardent work of the weaving of writing, then one would again come up against this scandal of the human condition, without being able to ward it off. The conspiratorial artifice of art is not – how simple that would be! – to bring the veracity of facts into the circle of our subjectivity, but to reveal the link, if there is one, woven between the latter and the former. It is with this 'if there is one' that rhetoric begins and writing runs its risk. Poetic art, the only imaginable form of 'exploration', is a phase of the possible.

In doing this, Michel Leiris is in no way either essentialist or nominalist. He does not intend to define. And the link between the inconceivable system of existence and the deliberate system of expression is neither fusion nor confusion. The meticulous eye is an eye that listens, oh Claudel,* *and speaks*. The confession is first of all a discourse, where wordplay, and the games of words, combine within each other. One could sum up the process like this: what existence has spread all around, discourse organizes. Or better: what the folding has concealed, poetics unfolds. From folding to unfolding, the movement is unceasing.

This to-and-fro also concerns objects, which are active witnesses and highly significant particles of the weave: 'Such a series of objects, spaced out like a flux, must necessarily see another series following it as its reflux' (p. 62). Leiris shares, but also goes beyond, the surrealists' passion for bric-à-brac, for the chance encounter of strange chosen objects, whose listing (the poetic argument of the exploration of the real) proceeds from the 'there is ...' of Guillaume Apollinaire.** For Leiris, such lists are reversible, reciprocally contaminating. Folding-unfolding.

*

When we say 'rhetoric', we do not mean a body of precepts cleverly activated nor a didactic ruse, but an adventurous dynamic of the word, a gamble laid bare, in the relation of outside-inside, self-world, existence-expression.

Leiris's prose is thus a meta-prose which at every moment evaluates its own level of expressibility (in those moments where the author 'confesses' the facts) and its levels of reflexibility, when the same author compares his confession to the equivalence that we have stated, from the *Haut mal* of life to the *Frêle bruit* of writing.

The complex stages of contamination, for example semantic, gradually tie the knot of the sentence, as in *Aurora* where the name of the heroine inaugurates a procession of derived meanings, OR AURA, OR AUX RATS, HORRORA, O'RORA, and where Leiris writes this, which prefigures many of the sequences in *La règle du jeu*:

> I reflected on what I had seen and, looking above the shed that had been turned into a mass grave towards the Polar star vaguely shining

---

*   Paul Claudel (1868–1955, French poet and dramatist, whose work reflected his Catholicism.
**   Guillaume Apollinaire (1880–1918), French poet, forerunner of Surrealism.

like the ironic point of Paracelsus's sword, I thought about the name Aurora, attached to the fate of that extraordinary girl whom the last fragments of clouds were now carrying towards a skyscraper built - with what everlasting cement? — on the edge of a continent that is extraordinarily stable and clear but also smoky, and I remembered that in Latin the word 'hora' means 'hour', that the root *or* appears in *os, oris* which means 'mouth' or 'orifice', that it was on Mount *Ararat* that the ark came to rest at the end of the flood, and finally that if Gérard Nerval* hanged himself one night in an obscure alleyway in the centre of Paris, it was because of two semi-ghostlike creatures who each bore one half of this name: Aurélia and Pandora. (p. 178)

These contaminations, along with many others, for example geographical ones (collusions between places), and always induced by the supra-logical mysteries of semantics, and many other kinds of transversalities, are explicitly related to the procedures of alchemy and transmutation: from existence to speech, from death-life to rhetoric, which alone excuses it and allows one to endure it.

Leiris's prose is a single long breathlessness, a crosshatching of breaths, strong or restrained, as of someone who, half suffocating, sees a mawkish apocalypse coming and tries to take its measure.

*

Already in *Aurora,* the evocation of the state that for Leiris was boredom, which is neither spleen nor melancholy, and which he admitted to feeling, to the friends who visited him in the final days of his life. He is bored when he is not pursuing the correlation between the refolding of existence and the unfolding of writing. I do not conclude that he lived in order to write, but certainly that writing did not satisfy him when he could not find in it material to support life. Boredom is that gaping hole that sometimes, in the open break between living and writing, spreads forth its gloomy indifference.

Thus he contrasted the shapeless mass of the lived with the rhythmical rigour of the rhetorical weave. *Aurora* tells us this, in its provocative and exaggerated manner:

---

*   Gérard Nerval (1808–1855), French Romantic poet.

For I must say that I have always associated life with what is sluggish, lukewarm and disproportionate. Liking only what is intangible, what is outside life, I arbitrarily identified everything hard, cold, or geometrical with that invariant, and that is why I like the angular lines that the eye projects into the sky to grasp the constellations, the mysteriously premeditated structure of a monument, and finally the ground itself, the site *par excellence* of all figures. (p. 82)

We know that, beyond this passion for geometrical figures, maps and topographical documents, so distant from what one would call the human, the work of Michel Leiris is an obstinate search for the only kind of weave that holds together, that which establishes a relation and enables us to overcome the sluggish, the lukewarm and the disproportionate, by lucid solidarity.

The final word of his rhetoric, having passed through the deferment of the real and the shifting of writing, indicates a true – liberated – relation to the Other.

The earth womb of the Caribbean countries, Haiti.

Who can never stop paying for her audacity in conceiving and raising up the first Negro nation in the world of colonization.

Who for two hundred years has felt what Blockade means, renewed each time.

Who suffers without respite her encampments and her mad sea, and grows in our imaginations.

Who has sold her Creole blood for half a dollar per litre.

Who has in turn distributed herself in the Americas, the Caribbean, Europe and Africa, remaking the diaspora.

Who has used up all her wood, marking her hills with arid wounds.

Who has founded a Painting and invented a Religion.

Who is always dying in the fighting between her black elites and her mulatto elites, both equally predatory.

Who has carried along beautiful or terrible words, the word *macoute*, the word *lavalass*, the word *déchouquer*.

The drum of the Whole beats in the poetry of Aimé Césaire:
Je me suis, je me suis élargi – comme le monde –
Et ma conscience plus large que la mer!
J'éclate. Je suis le feu, je suis la mer.
Le monde se défait. Mais je suis le monde.*
And flows in muffled surprises in the art of Saint-John Perse:
Et la mer à la ronde roule son bruit de crânes sur les grèves,
Et que toutes choses au monde lui soient vaines, c'est ce qu'un soir, au bord du monde, nous contèrent
Les milices du vent dans les sables d'exil ...**

Has it not been said, of this poet, that he went from the heartbeat of the Caribbean (*Éloges*) to the swell of the Pacific mixed with the High Plateaux of Asia (*Anabase*) to the misty spray of the Atlantic (*Exil*)? The seas flow in this wandering like abandoned rivers.

---

* 'I have, I have enlarged myself – like the world – And my consciousness larger than the sea! I burst open. I am the fire, I am the sea. The world falls apart. But I am the world'.
** 'And the sea all around rolls its noise of skulls on the shore, and its indifference to everything in the world is what, one evening, on the edge of the world, we were told by the militias of the wind in the sands of exile ...'

The body of Douve

When *Du mouvement et de l'immobilité de Douve* appeared,* there was quite a large group of us, poets living in France, of more or less the same age, who were interested in a broadening of poetic discourse, either on the horizons of a country and the world, in the case of Kateb Yacine, or in the exhalations of the stanza, considered as a measure of the human breath and a crucible of the noise of the world, as had been illustrated in turn by Segalen, Claudel and Saint-John Perse.

It would perhaps make a small contribution to the literary history of this period to show how this category of poets, whom nothing in fact 'brought together' – neither school nor theory nor manifesto – reacted to *Douve*. Among them, Jacques Charpier, whose poem *Connaissez-vous l'Écolière* was popular with us, Jean Laude who was to become a specialist in the detailed history of African Art and a poet whose ample darkness diffused whorls of patient light, and Roger Giroux whose first book of poetry, *L'Arbre le temps*, would later be published in the same edition of *Mercure de France* in which *Douve* appeared.

In some sense, poets involved with History, either because they had suffered its effects and challenged it (Yacine) or because they reflected on its contradictory meanings (Laude, Charpier). Or else, in the case of Roger Giroux or Paul Mayer, convinced by the same passion for rhetoric, in the writing sense of the word, which was the opposite of that absence, that sparseness of the word on the page that was beginning to take over poetic expression in France. And yet Giroux, a major poet, would later on incline more towards this silence, where nevertheless I can point to the breaks in his old way of writing. Pierre Oster held himself aloof. Jean Grosjean, even more distant, paced out his prophetic countryside.

Douve was far away from us, but totally present.

In the first place because of its dialectic – let's not be afraid of this word. The poet invites us to consider it, quoting Hegel as an epigraph to his text:
 'But the life of Spirit is not the life that shrinks from death and keeps itself untouched by devastation, but rather the life that endures it and maintains itself in it.'

---

* *Du mouvement et de l'immobilité de Douve*, Yves Bonnefoy, 1953.

The quotation appealed to the Hegelians that most of us were or wanted to be, and yet it contained a first, and very fleeting, ambiguity. It became easy to conceive of *movement* as life and to equate *immobility* with death. The text of the poem soon urged us to distance ourselves from such a crude mechanism.

Douve appealed to us as the first text by a poet of our generation who stated without stating that poetry is knowledge, even if this knowledge comes through what Bonnefoy would later call the improbable.

I think it was also the first book of contemporary poetry that we had regarded as being both total and so untotalitarian, and it was clear to us that the body of Douve, object of poetry, obscure and luminous, divided but always reconstituted, revealed itself as one and as transfigured by the multiplicity that ran through it.

Reading the poem, one could not help but return constantly to that shattered multiplicity of the body of Douve. I say the body, since Douve, who promises knowledge, does not offer herself under the auspices of pure evanescence. She is a secret knowledge *torn apart*, and which *breaks*, these are quotations from the poem, who sees her eyes *corrupted*, who is flooded with 'cold heads with beaks and jaws'.

Such distributions of the body of Douve lead one to think that she extends herself in the earth with a terrible impatience.

I came back to the book, where the image of this space was gradually woven together, this extension that was like an exploration both of oneself and outside oneself.

In order to recompose one of the fields, no, one of the directions, among others, I could see, let's say that I recognized, *the coal*, the charred land whose dead body carries and supports life, *the sand*, whose mobility is forever fixed, *the spider's web*, which is like sand taking on a shape, *the ivy*, canvas and sand and vegetal coal, and *the luxuriant grass*, which combines in its eagerness all life and all death.

An impressive variety, from coal to grass, a diversity that conforms to itself. All realities at the same time dense and woven. We understood why Douve was obscure and luminous, one and transfigured. It is because she did not think of herself as being exempt from the assaults of the earth, that she was truly telluric. To receive the blows of flint or thunder, to be in the grip of cold and shadow, made of her a very pure present. The knowledge that the poem offered passed through this unprotesting energy, which foreshadowed our own questions.

The text proudly refused to specify its circumstances. But one could follow the movement not of Douve but of the poet. He went from a multiple past:

Je te voyais courir sur les terrasses
Je te voyais lutter contre le vent ...

Towards an ineluctable present, or presents:

Je me réveille, il pleut. Le vent te pénètre, Douve, lande résineuse endormie près de moi ...

Was this not, way beyond time, the mark of a consciousness which, let's put it like this, makes itself History? And also, of an attempt to open up the thickness of the world? This poetry led to the meditation of Being, but through teaching the most insistent elements of the real.

Le ravin pénètre dans la bouche maintenant
Les cinq doigts se dispersent en hasards maintenant
La tête première coule entre les herbes maintenant
La gorge se farde de neige et de loups maintenant
Les yeux ventent sur quels passagers de la mort et c'est nous dans ce vent dans cette eau dans ce froid maintenant

A measured prosody, nothing superfluous or affected, a kind of severity of inspiration that would exclude the feeble exaltations that had previously excited the poem in France. But also, brusque rhythms, breaks, and often circularities where the poem rolls back on itself, turning it into a single river, a current that flowed from a quasi legendary past to this present time, struck with multiple splendour.

And, as though to pre-empt our surprise, the poet projected into the future what I can only, at this point in his meditation, call an *Art poétique*: this is the poem, prefiguring the poem as a whole, that he titles *Vrai nom*, and that I consider to be one of the most beautiful impulses of contemporary French poetry:

Je nommerai désert ce château que tu fus
Nuit cette voix, absence ton visage
Et quand tu tomberas dans la terre stérile
Je nommerais néant l'éclair qui t'a porté.

It is one of the truths of poetry that an *Art poétique* is always in the future, always marked with the sign of that which is to come. It is a promise by the poet, and it seems to me that Bonnefoy, in *Hier régnant désert* for example, has kept that promise. But also future in the sense that improbability devours the promise, and the unfinished never exhausts it.

The fire, the spirit, that shines darkly in Douve, we can if we want carry them deep within us, or on the contrary expose them to the wind of the world: in both cases they continue to burn and to achieve.

This is because the quivering weight of the presence and the obstinate elevation of thought are one and the same thing.

Que j'aime qui s'accorde aux astres par l'inerte
Masse de tout son corps,
Que j'aime qui attend l'heure de sa victoire,
Et qui retient son souffle et tient au sol.*

*

I have not spoken about death at all. Its dialectic had seemed to disappear beneath the body of the poem, the body of Douve. But it was this very promise of life, expressed so logically by Hegel, brought to fruition by Valéry in *Le Cimetière marin*, that was struck down and brought back to life in Douve, who illuminates it with so many radiant obscurities.

---

* Literal translations of the quotations from the poem are as follows: 'I saw you run on the terraces, I saw you struggle against the wind …'; 'I wake up, it's raining. The wind penetrates you, Douve, resinous moor sleeping beside me …'; 'The ravine enters the mouth now, the five fingers disperse in chances now, the head flows first between the grasses now, the gorge is decorated with snow and wolves now, the eyes blow on such passengers of death and it's us in this wind in this water in this cold now'; 'I will name this castle that you were a desert, night that voice, absence your face, and when you fall into the sterile earth I will name nothingness the lightning that carried you there'; 'How I love him who reaches out to the stars with the inert mass of his whole body, how I love him who awaits the hour of his victory, and holds his breath and clings to the ground'.

The tragic roughness of Kateb Yacine's work, the obstinate perseverance of his existence, have made him into a tormented, secret and luminous figure. He was never lost on the sidelines.*

---

* Kateb Yacine (1929–1989), Algerian poet and novelist who worked to promote the cause of the Berber people.

Mandela's Time

There are some times that are preserved, others that fade away. Nelson Mandela's time victoriously covered the coming of apartheid, the absolute system of horror, accentuated by its official title of 'separate development'. Absolute? Because the system was complete, everyday, both savage and petty, completely closed. In his autobiography Nelson Mandela says of it: 'The often haphazard segregation of the past three hundred years was to be consolidated into a monolithic system that was diabolical in its detail, inescapable in its reach and overwhelming in its power'.* And he describes this daily life: 'It was a crime to walk through a Whites Only door, a crime to ride a Whites Only bus, a crime to use a Whites Only drinking fountain, a crime to walk on a Whites Only beach, a crime to be on the streets after 11pm, a crime not to have a pass book and a crime to have the wrong signature in that book, a crime to be unemployed and a crime to be employed in the wrong place, a crime to live in certain places and a crime to have no place to live' (op. cit. vol. 1, p. 212). Without counting the desolate towns, those townships of mud and dust, usually without water or electricity or hygiene services; sordid conditions of existence, of health, of education, and this in one of the richest countries of the world (one thinks of the destitution of Zaïre, perched on so many underground resources), whose strategic importance is such that it seemed as though no help could have come from anywhere to overthrow this order of madness.

*

What has struck the imagination of the peoples of the earth: that in one life a man should have lived these irreconcilable, mutually inconceivable moments. The time when a little African boy is born in a tiny village in the Transkei, with no chance of escaping from the circuit of dependency and non-existence, the time when a militant is imprisoned for what seems to be an eternity, and the time when this same Rolihlahla ('*He who creates problems*') Mandela, who was given the Christian name Nelson, became – in April 1994 – president of the Republic of South Africa. He who has traversed this untrodden path seems to have had profound relations of complicity with Time.

---

* Nelson Mandela, *Long Walk to Freedom* [1994], (London: Abacus, 2002), vol. 1, p. 159.

As though some Power had kept him apart from the passing days until he, Mandela, was truly ready for another task, decided by the victorious struggle of the South African people. As if he had been kept in reserve, preserved (for twenty-five years of militant struggle, underground actions, experience of armed struggle, and for twenty-seven more years of prison, which was no less dangerous) for this moment when the world, in turn, would be ready to accept and to demand that this task should finally become concrete: a non-racial democracy, which the ANC had advocated from the start, and which for a long time had seemed, to both actors and spectators in this drama, to be an unrealizable dream.

*

Nelson Mandela sensed that he could have an influence on the passage of time, at the cost of so much suffering. 'In prison the minutes can seem like years, but the years go by like minutes. An afternoon pounding rocks in the courtyard might seem like forever, but suddenly it is the end of the year, and you do not know where all the months went' (op. cit. vol 2 p. 85.). Was he perhaps chosen by destiny (and can we believe in destiny?), he who survived where so many others, whom he names and honours in his work, have perished?

But he is, as he makes clear all along, a militant of the ANC, careful to respect the discipline of his party (in spite of a few lapses in the past, due to the enthusiasm of youth), faithful, obeying the decisions of the majority.

It is all the more surprising to learn how in the final years of his detention (about 1988–1989), when he is for the first time completely isolated from his companions, he dares to try to make contact with the government of Botha and then De Klerk, and tries hard to defend his point of view to the dispersed leadership of the ANC. His unfailing solidarity with Oliver Tambo who was at the time directing the organization from the outside (from Lusaka, in Zambia), and with Walter Sisulu, who for twenty years had been his companion in prison, probably facilitated the new direction taken by the ANC at this time. Nevertheless Nelson Mandela's almost solitary initiative seems to have been decisive. The thousands and thousands of deaths of members of the ANC and the other anti-apartheid organizations, the Blacks, Indians, Coloureds, Zulus and Whites who had supported their struggle and participated in it, had made it possible to win this war. Mandela's time is the time of the South African people.

This time leads to liberation ('The Whites in this country cannot go on being so blinded ... I always knew I would get out of prison' op. cit. vol. 2, p. 279), passing on the way through days and years: his youth in the landscape of the Transkei, the rituals of the Themba royal family (including a remarkable scene of circumcision), his difficult adolescence, the lawyers' firm opened in Johannesburg with Oliver Tambo (the first black lawyers' firm in South Africa), the daily experience of apartheid, membership of the ANC, mass struggles, arrests and trials, working underground, organizing the armed struggle, the enormous stretch of time, as though autonomous and singular, in prison, Soweto, the ANC's decision to make the prisoner Mandela a symbol, liberation, the elections, and victory.

*

Three-quarters of a century without any respite, punctuated by so much distress, death, suffering, joyfulness and hope. Narrated with the precision and humour of the African griot. Read how he describes Mrs Margaret Thatcher, lecturing him and telling him to cut down – 'at his age' – on his schedule of engagements, while he was on the world tour that followed his liberation. Mrs Thatcher was amazed that Mandela had such a heavy timetable.

*

And an unpretentious wisdom that resonates in simple statements: 'The curious beauty of African music is that it uplifts even as it tells a sad tale' (op. cit. vol. 2 p. 255).

*

Now President, the person who is in charge of business. One of the most decided, and decisive, men of Africa. Seeing him on the world's television screens, I have the feeling that he is keeping his distance, he who has intervened so much in reality. It is as though he is returning from a vertigo of time that has left absence on his face and has inclined him to a haughty and familiar good naturedness, with which he considers everything and everyone.

He has renounced nothing of his Themba and Xhosa roots, he is nostalgic for the country of his childhood, and he is also convinced that South African society can only be multiracial. The two feelings are not contradictory. It is not necessary to reject oneself in order to open up to the other. Fellow citizens can be different, without having to 'integrate' in order to work together, live together. From this the Nation takes on a new meaning.

Nelson Mandela is also discreetly capitalist in his opinions, but never anticommunist (it is a peculiarity of South African politics that the leaders of the Communist Party could have been members of the ANC or its leadership, without the two organizations merging together). He is happy to say that he is an Anglophile and to confide that he loves the films of Sophia Loren. A man who is free and diverse in his unity as a man.

*

The leaders of South Africa, who will have to satisfy the claims of so many dispossessed people and who will find themselves the target of the traps of international politics from which they will be able to extricate themselves, devote themselves to working for reconciliation in the country. (But it is said that criminality there is one of the highest in the world, that corruption is running wild, that the power of the Whites under apartheid has hardly been touched, and people are already shocked at the extent, in this fight against atrocity, of the atrocities committed in the name of the ANC.) If they succeed in this, they will have opened the twenty-first century with a worldwide burst of action and a promise of equilibrium. The Diversity of the world needs the South African experience, its success and what it can teach us.

*

Distant presence of this time of Mandela. Those of us who were young have grown up, we have gone from one project to another, we have achieved or not achieved our existences, we have watched mornings rise over the horizon of the sea, we have traversed the paths of our works, defended our causes, our children were there, we have discovered the world-totality and found ourselves deeply changed by it, and in the distance this presence has always remained intact in the movement of everything.

It had seemed to us that we had not recognized the slow, patient mission of Mahatma Gandhi until the moment he fell under the assassin's bullets. That we had hardly heard of Martin Luther King when he too was killed. That the destiny of Che Guevara had run its course before he contributed so greatly to changing our sensibilities. As if for us, spectators of the world's drama, these figures belonged to death, when it is life itself that gives itself up to be reborn in other lives.

But we felt Mandela's time growing in the distance. A time that involved both the instant and duration. (It was like a heavy, round, full time, waiting to unleash itself. We can compare it to the time of Yasser Arafat, equally indefatigable, who seems for such a long time not to have completed his work and to be lost in the infinity of the sands of Gaza.) And when the elections brought him to the Presidency of his country, it was as though the door of the Sun, white and black and red and yellow in the early morning, had opened onto the future of the world. We could then be sure that Mandela's time had always been in contact with ours. Through all these times that cross and navigate our waves and our backwashes like the skiffs and fishing boats of the wind, he had kept himself ready to let us know finally that nothing of the unpredictability of the world is impossible in future.

We think of the West (in the West) as the place of the Rights of Man, of freedom of judgement, which we like to contrast with the fantastical rigidity of Islam. What stupidity. Judaism, Christianity and Islam all share the same spirituality of the One and the same belief in a revealed Truth. Three monotheistic religions, which grew up around the Mediterranean basin and which have all three engendered absolutes of spirituality and heights of exclusion, elevations of supreme intensity, and, equally, the same fundamentalisms, each in turn exacerbated. In this sense, Islam is one of the remarkable components of the West that has spread across the world, exactly as the Christian kingdoms did, even if it was in different ways. The thought of the One, which has brought such greatness, has also distorted so much. How can we accept this thinking, which transfigures, without thereby offending against or turning away from the Diverse? For it is diversity that protects us and, perhaps, allows us to continue.

The Book of the World.

The book is threatened with physical disappearance (this is one of our best-known common places), for all sorts of reasons which come down to this: the advances of the audiovisual and of computerization are unstoppable and fiercely discriminatory. That is what people say.

The time has passed in which we could dream of or design the world as a totality but a conceivable one, one whose future development we could conceptualize as a desirable harmony. The future development that we can conceive of now is that of the unfinishable. We are forever being seduced by the unpredictable and the discontinuous. All published books are judged by what will be the next one to appear, by what its form will be, or by being projected into the space of our thought like a virtual reincarnation.

Towards the end of his life Stéphane Mallarmé,* piling up notes, corrections and documents to this end, wanted to accomplish the Book that would finally mean everything and transcend everything. But in Mallarmé's time the world in itself had already begun to carry out its ramblings; it was already combatting that purification of knowledge that he wanted - that quest for essence - with an irreducible diversity, which elsewhere Victor Segalen was to establish as a principle of poetics.

They both shared a similar Intention, which was to posit a Measure against the immeasurable, a rhythm of knowledge against all the unknowable in the world, and to contain this disorder and this multiplicity by the rhetorical regulations that they had at their disposition.

But the world had moved further on, as world and as totality. It is as though these poets had guessed from above or through vertigo the bewildering jumble of this diversity: Mallarmé as dreamer of Being, Segalen troubled by being, fragile, caught up in its unpredictability.

And if Mallarmé had realized his Book, which would have been the Book of the world, then any kind of book would have vanished from our horizons, both as project and as object.

*

The unpredictable and the discontinuous delight us, even though we are afraid to accustom ourselves to their spiral. If the techniques of the visual,

---

*   Stéphane Mallarmé (1842–1898), symbolist poet.

of computing and of orality are changing the substance of books, even if they replace them with strange objects that we cannot imagine, if they transform libraries into something quite different from media centres, even if they push traditional books – i.e. those that have not been filmed - back into their depths, where they must be explored at length, does it necessarily mean that this filming has broken their spell or dimmed their brightness? Does the transparency of the screen not equate to the thickness of the page? And will we not get used to these strange objects?

Let us say this: the internet, which we choose as symbol and model for the moment, throws us right into the unfurling of our world-totality, and it would seem, even if we can click back onto a previous subject, that we cannot step twice into the same water, that the literality of the world is for us both actuality and fleetingness, that we cannot keep hold of anything that would anchor us, in this perpetual current. Or else must we also learn how to learn without holding onto anything?

You will object that the internet is more like a stock, an accumulation, than a flow of water. This is true. But the way we use it determines its characteristics. When we consult it, we are always moving. If the classical sciences worked on the infinitely small and the infinitely large, we sense that computer science (it already exists) considers only that which is infinitely moving.

The book, as project and object, allows me to gamble on finding every time that same water on my skin. Its current brings me to the spring and the delta, its beginning and its end, and in any case however many pages I want at the same time, it leaves me free to imagine them all together: what it stretches out between its banks is a proof of its permanence. Or else, should we learn to discover permanence, or at least the taste for permanence, in the unceasing movement of the literal? I would put it like this: the internet unfolds the world, it offers it in all its weight, while the book illuminates and delivers its invariants.

*

Why should I still connect myself to invariants? Is this not the appropriate disguise that the old phantom of the absolute would choose to clothe itself in? Is the literal reality of the Chaos-world not sufficient to satisfy all fantasies, desires or aspirations? To be delirious in delirium, carnivalesque in carnivals, savage in savagery? But even if I accustom my sensibility to the unexpectedness of the Chaos-world, and accept that I should no longer try to plan it or predict it in order to rule it, the fact remains that I will not be able to accompany it in its course if I am totally carried away by it. Someone caught up in a maelstrom can neither see nor think about the maelstrom. This is why an art based on literalness, an elementarism or a realism, would not put me in a position to experience the world, to approach it or to know it; it would allow me only to passively undergo it.

The invariant is very similar to what we have said about the common place: a place in which one thought of the world meets another thought of the world. Focal points in the turbulence, that enable me to dominate or tame my anxiety, my present fear, my vertigo.

The immeasurability of the world can be explored through the immeasurability of the text, and it is by revealing the invariants of the former, the fleeting encounters, the relevances of the relations, what brings together the silences and the bursts of noise, that the latter does more than drearily reproduce it literally.

The thrust of the invariants does not found an Absolute, it establishes Relation. Between here and elsewhere, inside and outside, myself and the other, clay and granite. In this weave the poet inscribes his intention, the pursuit of the poem or the phases of its recital. The book is a crucible in which all this is transmuted. It allows for stopping, for the foundation of the present time, for populating, through the divination of the invariants and the fulfilment of the intention. It de-literalizes the immeasurability of the world, but without losing its impact or trying to neutralize it.

*

Our practice or our sharing of languages passes through so many experiences of the everyday, so many chance contacts, so many illuminations immediately reduced to a fleeting gleam of light. But the text preserved as a book gives us the poetic leisure to entrust to it our *langage*, even if this has been forged in orality.

The use of languages suits the table of the internet. The alchemy of *langage* requires this crucible of the book, even though we hastily throw into it materials that we hope will be transsubstantiated. The speed and the fulguration proper to the book are not the same as those that carry us away when we are in front of the computer screen. The latter result from a prodigious accumulation, the former from a deferment suddenly revealed. Language grows only through *langage*, that mark of the poet, and *langage* needs all languages, which are the imagination of the world.

*

And, similarly, we actually read in these two ways. One in languages, one in *langage*.

The first is erratic. An advertisement on a street corner, a thriller that suddenly shows us violence (a major invariant of our time), a broadsheet philosophy, no more absurd than any other, a popular novel, a fashionable work, the confession of a serial criminal, an essay on the truffles of Périgord and how to dig them up or on Moroccan couscous and its juicy sweetness, worrying banalities on the emotion of death, fragments, scattered accumulations, we should be noting all this, we don't have time, it is like the root running to meet other roots, like the leaf mingling with other leaves, we actually read what we hear on television or what fascinates us in the cinema, all the presence of all the languages that we use, a disjointed reading, naively ferocious, a piling up of flashes of light, of communications, which we do not join up together, you can't join up flashes of light, it is indeed the Whole-World that we are dealing with without knowing it, we let it appear and disappear within us, but its work goes on, we gradually learn to distinguish those invariants that it is so necessary for us to know, and once again we put off the process of ordering this knowledge, and in this way we descend (as though literally) into the letter of the world.

Then, we pause, we claim the right to rest. We go back to the great texts, to what are called the great texts, and there, generally speaking, we prefer the big books, the books of duration, which give us time, the Chinese *Water Margin*,* *The History of the Decline and Fall of the Roman Empire* or *La littérature européenne et le Moyen Âge latin*.** This is because we are now thinking about our *langage*.

---

* *The Water Margin*, attributed to the Chinese writer Shi Na'ian (*c*.1296–1327).
** *La littérature européenne et le Moyen Âge latin*, Ernst Robert Curtius, 1948.

With the first kind of reading, we are attending to the world, we are experiencing its multiplicity, we are caught up in it. But with the second? What are we seeking in these fundamental texts, beyond the slow, measured pleasure of perceived beauty? In this duration that seems to take us away from the bustle of the world?

My guess is that we are there in a state of medium-ness. We are perhaps searching above all for the harbingers of the totality that now calls to us. We want to find our invariants in it, and we ask how these texts have been able to foresee them. To reinforce in ourselves, against the discontinuous vagaries of precious wandering, the sense of duration, the rough patience of time. This is what I call prospecting our own *langage*. Yes. That is how we read these big books.

And for example, we find, in the abrupt, fragmentary texts of the pre-Socratics – as though the fragment were a piece of a vanished duration – this feeling that our period has renewed that pre-Socratic era, when the hybridities of islands, the archipelagic thinking and the dreams of the Great-Whole had connected the human to the earthly, or the cosmic. We imagine that we are beginning again that encounter, at least as long as we are not afraid of its mystical excesses. And that is an invariant.

We realize, from the slow history of Chaka as told by Thomas Mofolo and based on the stories of the Zulu people, that the epic heroes are almost all bastards who must painfully found a legitimacy that belongs to them alone, but that they are almost always harmed by their descendants. And that is an invariant.

We follow, as though along a river that appears and disappears, how the Amerindian myths and stories signify that the earth never becomes property, that it cannot be a territory, that human communities are not its masters, that man is its guardian, not its absolute owner. (We remember that when asked why they wear shoes whose toes turn up in front, like medieval shoes or Saracen boots, the traditional Mongolian wrestlers reply: 'It's so as not to hurt the earth'.) And that is an invariant.

With the first reading we collect, in a disorganized fashion, the material of the world; we do it in waves, like a population of scurrying ants. A reading by city-dwellers, people vulnerable to the busy streets and the mechanisms of communication, transport, socially organized work and leisure. A reading by agitated people who give themselves up to the flux. With the second, we isolate ourselves from the noise of the world but in order to find its trace or its invariant. A reading by country-dwellers, people who dream of a shack open to the wind of Morne-Rouge, or of a hearth, a fire, a chimney lost in a county, or of such slow discussions under the baobab tree as the sun slowly sets, all places in which one can be alone or else come together intentionally, a reading by people who think about their *langage*, serious and intense like the owl of Greece flying at dusk or the buffalo of Madagascar that no colony of leeches can disturb.

*

And here are those who, still today, have no chance of ever opening a book. Those who only ever experience a single Season, the *Saison en enfer*.* Who would only ever be able to discover a single invariant, that which knots inextricably together destitution, oppression, genocide, epidemics, mass graves, exclusion. Those who could neither distinguish or choose between life in the city or in the countryside, because they live permanently in the wastelands of life. Those who have no reason to fear the hypothetical ravages of audiovisual or computer techniques. For whom the book is still a mirage and, if it is there, a miracle.

I see again in my memory the primer of an Andean ethnic group, an irreplaceable book, spelling out the elements of a language under threat, lost in the silence of the mountain, on reddish brown coarse-grained paper, a book both humble and imperious in its necessity, perhaps already useless. The great libraries of the world will not be kept or preserved unless we also increase the number of small ones buried in the earth of the planet.

It is also true, as has been pointed out to me, that the Internet appears to be the instrument of the pre-eminence of technological societies over all others. In this respect, it has purely and simply replaced the book. In this huge creolization of cultures that it enables and inaugurates, the voices of the destitute are absent. We must reject this selective creolization, but still accept that it is advancing.

Will we one day be able to project into the space in front of us the verses of Homer (both in Greek and in translation, to make it more beautiful)? Probably. At least for those who will be able to master these techniques.

---

* *Une Saison en enfer* (A Season in Hell) is one of the major works of the poet Arthur Rimbaud (1854–1891).

But will we be able to compose poems, illustrate a creole language, weave a *langage*, in this suspended space? Write in the wind, create out of movement itself, turn a trap or a mishap into a patiently written work? Our attachment to the book replies that we cannot, our passion for the world claims that we can.

*

Let us open in us this book of the world, typographic or computerized. The poets' task is to bring us to this. But not Mallarmé's Book, absolute and improbable, not that Measure of immeasurability of which he so generously dreamed, but Immeasurability itself, unpredictable and unfinished. Let us not fear the unstoppable progress of the new techniques or the mutations that they cause in us.

I see the flux increasing and Relation in action.

But like you I am careful not to succumb to it completely. When the murmuring of the world takes hold of us, when it swells around us with so many diffracted decipherings, so many assaults of which we are barely conscious, when it subjugates or disperses us, we still know that we have in us that solitary buffalo, unassailable in its solidarity with us.

Thus the poet in his poem does not imitate immeasurability senselessly, he does not repeat it, rather he juxtaposes it with the immeasurability of his text, which is of a different kind. This is the moment when the noise slows down, while remaining present.

Let us spy on the murmuring.

It invades us, incessant internet and inexhaustible torrent, it overwhelms us with its vibration but - wait, look, listen - after it has filled us with all kinds of happiness and misery, it moves away and disappears, leaving us free to open the book we have chosen at the page that we want, or to write on this sheet of paper, which will soon be the page of a book, the first words of the poetics that we have always cared about, and then, this murmuring of the world, like a book that one closes or a poem that one begins to recite, it suddenly moves away into the distance, it leaves us, doubtless to reach other poems, rejoin and designate other common places, other invariants, and for us it fades away and, beautifully, dies out.

Which, redone in a pedagogical fashion, to be inserted into a CD-Rom on the book for example, and taken together with what we have said previously on writing (oh the pleasures of repetition) would give the following, which takes us to the joy of the common place:

Reading and Writing Today
Everyone agrees that the book is threatened by the progress of audio-visual techniques. One can indeed assume that we will soon have at our disposal devices that will project the texts that we wish to consult into space or onto the walls of our rooms. And even, that we would be able to put on the headset that would allow us to enter into virtual reality and to experience directly the scenes of the battle of Waterloo that open *La Chartreuse de Parme*, or to find ourselves in the cell with Edmond Dantès and the abbey Faria, preparing to relive for ourselves the escape that inaugurates the adventures of the *Count of Monte-Cristo*.

Science fiction authors have imagined the time when books would therefore be abandoned in Libraries, which would become deconsecrated cathedrals and where those who continued to consult these strange works would be considered weirdoes, or ill in some way, who would meet up almost clandestinely in underground places, rather like the first Christians in the catacombs, to hastily and feverishly leaf through an original edition of the *Chants de Maldoror* or a miraculously preserved collection of *La Petite Illustration*, a magazine that was fashionable in France and the French colonial empire in the 1930s. In this way, the audiovisual would have killed reading, rendering it superfluous, and would have signed the death warrant of the book.

One can also judge that the book and the computer screen complement each other. Use of the latter gives us the vertiginous accumulation of the world's data, and the fastest possible way of putting them in correlation with each other. Knowledge in general, the science or sciences more particularly and technically, need these new practices. Our leisure activities, our search for pleasure and relaxation, will be changed by it. The common place, thus reshuffled, protects us from confusion when faced with the absolutely new.

But could it not be that this very speed, which is so invaluable, constitutes a lack? In our increasingly accelerated dealings with the diversity of the world, we need pauses, times for meditation, where we step aside from the flood of information that is provided for us so that we can start putting some order into our accidental encounters. The book is one of these moments. After the first period of excitement, of limitless appetite for the new means of acquiring knowledge that computer technology affords us, it is good to find a balance, and for reading to regain its function of stabilizing and regulating our desires, our aspirations, our dreams. The common place, as exemplified above, generally helps us to accept the oppositions and encourages us to reconcile them.

This distribution of roles recurs in the very manner in which we read today. One kind of reading grabs our attention, rapid, everyday, and almost unconscious. An advertising placard at the corner of a street, a newspaper article, a thriller, fragments of information on the happenings of the world: a choppy, rushed reading, as though we were in an Internet that swiftly supplied us with a sparkling series of pieces of information.

Another kind of reading, which we perform in a far more thoughtful manner, when we are at home, and we have the time to choose. Then, we are not afraid of big books, which take some time to read: *War and Peace*, *In Search of Lost Time* or Plutarch's *Parallel Lives*.

We do not take the same books onto the bus or the tram, or in the dizzying local taxis of Martinique. We who have the leisure to read instinctively know how to organize our readings. This corresponds to the two ways in which we employ our thinking: to experience the world by being in it, even if we are sometimes carried away by its complexity and its rapidity; or else to reflect on our relation to the world, on its transformations outside us and in us, on the future that it offers us. In the first case, we do not separate our readings from our daily activities, we are in the unceasing Internet of life. In the second case, we isolate ourselves, we seek the silence and the concentration of someone meditating on his future, we are in the permanence and the slow work of the book. Is this prejudice ('good' and 'bad' literature) or a necessary division?

These same considerations are also valid for the practice of writing. Writing today is not simply a case of telling stories to amuse or move, or to impress, it is above all perhaps to look for the reliable link between the crazy diversity of the world and the balance and knowledge that we wish for in ourselves. This world is there in our consciousness or our unconscious, a Whole-World, and, whatever we say, it demands our attention more every day and we are obliged to try to test our abilities against it. The writer and the artist have asked us to do this. Their work is marked by this vocation.

To be aware of the totality of the world and of what it has caused to emerge in modernity. For example, knowledge of or desire for the other cultures and other civilizations, which complement our own. The importance of the techniques of orality, which are invading the practice of writing. The presence of the languages of the world, which inflect and alter the way in which each of us uses his own language. A whole mixture of possibilities for the artist and the writer, in which it is both exciting and difficult to choose one's way and to keep up the creative effort.

As a result of diversity, the writer is gradually abandoning the old division into literary genres, which in the past contributed to the emergence of so many masterpieces in the novel, the essay, poetry, drama. The explosion of this diversity and the speedy development of audiovisual and computer techniques have opened up the field to an infinite variety of possible genres, of which we do not yet have a complete conception. Readers (in countries where one has the leisure to read) are increasingly growing to like these mixtures of genres, novels that are historical treatises, biographies that, while still being accurate and detailed, are like novels, treatises on natural science or astrophysics or marine science that read like poems or meditations or adventure stories. Meanwhile, the poetics that have appeared in the world are gaily reinventing the genres, unrestrainedly mixing them up.

We write in the same way that we read, today. In a crazily active and rushed way, in tune with this whole momentum of the world and with the runaway progress of the techniques of modernity, which carry us along in their unstoppable flux. And perhaps, then, the writer becomes a provider of the Internet's floods. We also prepare, in oral accounts that are often hasty, incomplete with regard to our intention, given in the most diverse places, on dates that soon get mixed up, and like spot checks or letting off rockets or topographical snapshots, material that we will later withdraw into ourselves to organize on the page, when, while remaining in solidarity with the movement, we want to be solitary, just as the reader isolates himself. And in this case, the writer demonstrates all the patience that he needs in his work, for he sees in front of him the book that he will finish, and which he cannot imagine that human communities will one day no longer need.

I call the Whole-World our universe as it changes and lives on through its exchanges and, at the same time, the 'vision' that we have of it. The world-totality in its physical diversity and in the representations that it inspires in us: so that we are no longer able to sing, speak or work based on our place alone, without plunging into the imagination of this totality. The poets always foresaw this. But they were damned, those in the West, for not having accepted in their time the exclusivity of place, when this was the sole norm that was required. Damned also, because they were well aware that their dream of the world prefigured or accompanied its Conquest. The conjunction of the histories of peoples opens up for today's poets a new way of writing. Worldness, while it is attested in the oppressions and exploitations of the weak by the strong, is also to be found and experienced by poetics, far from any generalization.

It is the rhizome of all places that makes up the totality, and not a uniformity of place in which we would evaporate. Our earth, our share of the Earth, should not be constituted by us as a territory (of the absolute) from which we would believe ourselves authorized to conquer the places of the world. We are well aware that the forces of oppression are aimed everywhere and nowhere, that they are quietly corrupting our reality, that they govern it without us being able to see how or from where. But at least we can already combat them with the bright light of Relation, whereby we refuse to reduce a place or to make of it a Centre closed in on itself. Everyone is embarking, at every moment, on a Treatise on the Whole-World. There are a hundred thousand billions of them, rising up everywhere. Each time different in sea spray and soil. In Guadeloupe or Valparaiso, you leave from Baffin Island, or the land of Sumatra or the bungalow *Mon repos*, first turning after the Post Office, or, if your silt has crumbled around you, from a line that you have sketched out in the spaces, and you rise to that knowledge. The painter Matta again: *Toute histoire est ronde comme la terre. N'occidentons plus tout du long, orientons vraiment.**

---

* 'Every history is round like the Earth. Let us not westernize all the way, let us easternize/orientate.'

That the being is relation, and it goes everywhere. That human cultures exchange while living on, change without losing themselves: that this becomes possible. I am this mangrove country in the Lamentin in Martinique where I grew up and at the same time, thanks to an imperceptible infinite presence, which takes nothing away from the Other, that bank of the Nile where the reeds turn to bagasse like sugar canes. The aesthetic of Relation reduces to anachronism the illusions of exoticism, which made everything uniform.

Punctuations

Through so many crises that are the deadly price of coming together, through so many wars where the One has been confronted via its all too human incarnations, the Mediterranean is once again becoming an archipelago, returning to what it perhaps was before finding itself engaged with History. The Pacific Ocean and the Caribbean are seas that have always been archipelagos. The continents, those masses of intolerance rigidly turned towards a Truth, in so much as they regroup into entities or confederate in common markets, are also archipelagizing into regions. The regions of the world become islands, isthmuses, peninsulas, advances, lands of mixing and passage, yet which still remain.

Jacques Berque and Literatures

We agree, with surprise, that we are now witnessing an opening up of the word to the dimension of the world and that the supreme object of literature is precisely this world-totality.

The opening up does not imply the dilution of the voice in a vague Universal, nor a way of being nowhere, nor, for the being, a suspension, existence in suspense, nor a painful or gnawing erasure.

What we see and feel is that the place from which we utter the word, from which the voice makes itself heard, is all the more welcoming to their accents for being placed in Relation, opening up its subject matter, questioning its limit, destabilizing its limits.

In this way the poem forms a weave between the density of the place and the multiplicity of the diverse, between what is said here and what is heard over there. This is part of the jousting of the literary approach: to have to consult the unpredictability and the non-given of the world, through the fragile but persistent substance of our present, our surroundings.

There is a trajectory of wandering, from the place to the totality, and vice versa. The work does not go out into the world without returning to its source. This to-and-fro movement marks its true parabola. And Jacques Berque* teaches us this, each time that he has had to sum up his work, sketch out its general lines, its results. Whether it is about Islam, the Arab world, the West or the peoples of what used to be called the Third World, his detailed analyses never lose touch with a global vision: their conjunction allows him to study the episode of each day and to project the work of the future. He has always conceived of the approach to the Other *in* a vision of solidarity with the world.

I also realize (and he pointed it out himself) that when we met it was always to share a trembling, tiny or revelatory, physical or social or political, of the totality of the earth. Once in Florence, when the left-wing Catholic candidate La Pirra had just been elected mayor. In Algiers, the day of the Declaration of the Algerian Republic. In my home in Martinique, when a cyclone was about to pass over our heads and we stood at the window breathing the smell of lead and speculating on all those clouds that formed a blockade in the sky. Different places, but tethered to the same concern,

---

* Jacques Berque (1910–1995) was an Islamic scholar and sociologist.

governed by the same hope. The hope of a bright spell to come, the threat of an uncontrollable excess.

It is as though we had to repeat, all of us together, in the hazards of our existence, this common place of the intellectual and creative life of our time: to roam the imagination of the world to come to the debate of our own surroundings, or vice versa.

If the multiple root is missing, we are projected into an infertile space; but if the root closes up, encroaches, then we are blind to ourselves and to the world.

All the work that Jacques Berque has done on Islam, the Arab world, the colonized countries, also served to reflect on his own needs. So he saw in Islam its rationality but also its mystique. What does this mean, if not that that he believed that every conceptualization has its corresponding poetics? In the same way, he explained, through the subjects he studied, the often conflictual but always enriching encounter of orality and writing, in the double field of the Arabic language for example, but also in the context of modernity. All questions that are prominent in the literatures of today. He was one of the first in France to teach this, calmly, without any manifesto, with rectitude and clarity.

This clarity, in the structure of his thought and also in its expression, is close to what we could call a humanism. A clarity that is forever questioning. That of the pioneer, who clears the ground, or the ploughman. It is therefore also accompanied by an appeal to that which is blurred, to mystery, and by an anxious attention to whatever is weaving itself in the underside of the real, by an approach to the incomprehensible, the inexpressible.

Which does not in any way detract from its clarity.

*

Examiner of the disparities in the world, sensitive to its diversity, careful to emphasize its convergences, Jacques Berque gave us a privileged introduction to the literatures of the peoples of our time.

The Subject of Africa

The poetry of Léopold Sédar Senghor,* ceremonial and splendid, brings us the rhythm of the verse, in which we find our breath, and we will not forget that it has also fulfilled a function, humble and proud, regulated by the scribe or the copier, whereby it has brought African subject matter into the knowledge and sensibility of the beginning of the twentieth century.

It is not of course the dazzling science, the divination by thunder, that the Romans practiced literally and that was re-established in literature by the 'poètes maudits', Arthur Rimbaud or Antonin Artaud, but the patient requisition of a whole area of reality that is knocking at the doors of the world, at these multiple windows that are now opening onto our common modernities.

*

A solemn repertoire. The transfiguration, the offering of a whole universe, that of the cultures of black sub-Saharan Africa, up until then trapped in the complacencies that the forces of oppression spread in order to manage their impudent violations.

The scribe is not a clerk with fearless hands and a cold heart, and poetry never rejects this kind of encyclopedic work that is worthy of its most secret intention, a work of reorganizing and collecting together the given, through which it brings us close to the world's diversity, which we need so much. The poem is one of the matrices of the alchemy of the real.

The copyist is not the unflinching imitator, who would never depart from the model that he has chosen, and whose hand fills in the outlines of other people's drawing with monochrome colours. Léopold Sédar Senghor was suspected of having been as it were frozen by Catholic inspiration: a kind of paralysis in the face of the statue of the Commander in the shape of Claudel for example. But his model is African and, beneath the solemnity of the forms, the colours change according to the movement of the rivers and the assaults of the bush of the black country.

---

* Together with Césaire, Senghor was the founder of the Negritude movement.

*

In Senghor we find that sacred bestiary, which suddenly escapes the conventions of exoticism: those reptiles of the Third Day, those agami birds, those monkeys whose cries are like cymbals. Beasts that sing like omens, in this day of annunciation. They are seen and respected by the eye of memory, of tradition and intimate legend, by the eye that interprets.

Beasts, and also trees, ardently meeting up with those of Victor Segalen and Saint-John Perse, across spaces still unknown and not yet joined together.

Let us explore this newly established geography, which is no longer the prey of the discoverers and the conquerors but the tender place of lovers, the object of hard work, the interjection of suffering and joy, which are added on to the real. Colonization has not carried everything away in its derision.

The emotion of meeting the *kori*, which we are told is a 'thin line of greenery which, in the desert, marks the bed of a river, usually dried up', or of running along the *tann*, 'flat land covered by the sea or an inlet at the time of spring tides'. We carry within us our own *koris*, memories of ancient prosperity, and our *tanns*, promises of future fervour. This poetic geography announces sharing and Relation.

*

Let us learn, from the register of instruments of art as well as the catalogue of everyday tools. In this first half of the century, here are – offered and officiating – those objects that will become so familiar to music lovers, the kora and the balafon, and the *khalam*, quieter, 'a kind of four-stringed guitar, which is the usual accompaniment of the elegy'.

*

Africa! Africa! Country of colonialist tumult and devastation, but also country of the elegy, the *sabar* and the *mbalakh*, and of the *woy*, a song or poem, which the humanist Senghor realizes is 'the exact translation of the Greek ode'.

It may be that we do not willingly subscribe to this image of the Greco-Latin Negro, but do we not, ultimately, like the fact that Senghor, the son of prestigious and very ancient cultures, tries in this way to share with Western man what the latter has uttered most profoundly? Shall we deny the *woy* its kinship with the ode, and vice versa?

Around these poems, a human community rises. Samana Ban Ana Baâ for instance, who is quite a joker, and Koli Satiguy, a holy man, or Abou Moussa, the usurper.

African names will from now on proclaim their genealogy in the song of the world.

Bestiary, account of kinship, catalogue, botanical textbook, planisphere and portolan of the Senegalese country, Senghor's poetic world, more than it seemed, opened the way for the novelists and film-makers who have explored the reality of this part of Africa and have revealed its true riches.

*

A world strewn with angry shouts, punctuated by the sacred *tutoiement* of the fundamental texts, and where the spoken word is truly the elder sister of writing. Senghor's work is one of the first in which the traditional ease of African speech, solemn and joking, mocking or tragic, has informed the austere presence of the written poem.

It is not for me to point out that the work of the politician, the man of reflection and action, has met with objections and criticism: it is for the Senegalese people themselves to measure the distance that may have grown up between Senghor and them, to calculate the distance between Casamance and Normandy, which became the poet's favourite place, and to decide whether this distance is significant or not.

I like the fact that the calm insurrection of Senghor's words accompanied from the outset another exclamation, that of Aimé Césaire, and that the same new phase of the world came into being through these two representatives of Negritude: the man from the African source, the man from the diaspora.

The source moved elsewhere and Africa flowed into the Americas, after the holocaust of transportation. The Immense Waters of the Ocean drew them horribly together. Permanence has turned into diversity. Is this not what we sense in Senghor, when he confides in us, as though in a whisper: 'My heart is always wandering, and the sea has no limits.'

I am also happy to remind you, very briefly, that another Senegalese intellectual, Alioune Diop, undertook to list, in the review *Présence africaine*, the same concrete and significant particularities of the black country as Senghor's poem had pointed out. *Présence africaine* and *La Société africaine*, on which Senghor, Richard Wright, Cheik Anta Diop, Aimé Césaire, Frantz Fanon, Jacques Rabemananjara, and so many others collaborated.

Raise our voices for the bard that we see there serene and impassive. But his voice thrills with the trembling of his native land.

Globalization, seen as non-place, would indeed result in a standardized dilution. But for each of us, the path that leads from our place to the world and back again, again and again, indicates the only permanence. The world in its finished totality cannot be considered a sufficient reason, a generality giving birth to its own generalization. The weave of the world is enhanced by all the particularities, quantified; by all the places, recognized. The totality is not what has been called the universal. It is the quantity, finished and realized, of the infinite detail of the real. And which, because it is a matter of detail, is not totalitarian.

*The Earth and the Territory**

The 'realization' of the earth-totality has changed the perception or the imagination that each human community has of 'its' land. The physical frontiers between nations have been made permeable to cultural and intellectual exchanges, to the hybridization of sensibilities, which has meant that the nation-state is no longer powerful enough to barricade from the inside everyone's relation to *the earth.*

This does not cause a dilution of nationality, but a reduction in the number of nationalisms, in spite of the current excesses which, in the world, are the vehement sign of a return of the nationalist repressed.

The Poetics of Relation enables us to approach the difference between a land, which we relate to elsewhere, and a territory, whose doors we close to the wind blowing outside. Modernity swings uncontrollably between these opposite ways of our inhabiting of the place.

Summary of the Paper Given on This Occasion

I call creolization the meeting, the interference, the shock, the harmonies and disharmonies between cultures, in the realized totality of the world-earth.

Its characteristics are:
– the dizzying speed of the interactions that it sets up;
– the 'consciousness of consciousness' that we have of these;
– the mutual valorization that results and that makes it necessary for everyone to re-evaluate for themselves the components placed in contact (creolization does not presuppose a hierarchy of values);
– the unpredictability of the results (creolization is not limited to hybridity, whose syntheses were foreseeable).

The examples of creolization are inexhaustible and one observes that they first took shape and developed in archipelagic rather than continental situations.

My proposition is that today the whole world is archipelagizing and creolizing itself.

In these circumstances, it has become necessary for us to distinguish between two forms of culture:

Those that I will call atavistic, whose creolization took place a very long time ago, if it did take place, and which have meanwhile armed themselves

---

* Paper given at a conference on modernity at the University of Tokyo, November 1996.

with a corpus of mythical narratives aiming to reassure them as to the legitimacy of their relations with the land that they occupy. These mythical narratives usually take the form of a Creation of the world, of a Genesis.

Those that I will call composite, whose creolization is happening so to speak before our very eyes. These cultures do not generate a Creation of the world, they do not consider the founding myth of a Genesis. Their beginnings proceed from what I call a digenesis.

We observe that the composite cultures are tending to become atavistic, that is, to lay claim to a permanence, an honorability of time, which would seem to be necessary to any culture in order for it to be sure of itself and to have the boldness and the energy to express itself. They usually do this under the pressure of the necessities of their liberation (these cultures having almost all been the object of a colonization, violent or 'discreet'), which demands the passionate certainty that one is oneself and not someone else.

The atavistic cultures, in contrast, are tending to break up, to creolize themselves, that is, to question (or to defend very dramatically) their legitimacy. They do this under the pressure of the generalized creolization whose object, we have said, is the earth-totality.

This results in two conceptions of identity, which I have tried to define according to the image of the single root and the rhizome, developed by Deleuze and Guattari.

A sublime and deadly conception, which the cultures of Europe and the West have transported around the world, of identity as the single root, excluding the Other. The single root implants itself in a land that becomes a territory.

A notion that has now become 'real', in all composite cultures, of identity as rhizome, going to meet other roots. And that is how the territory once again becomes a land.

Among the myths that have led the way towards the consciousness of History, the foundational myths have had as their role to consecrate the presence of a community on its land, by attaching this presence to a Genesis, without any discontinuity and by legitimate filiation. This is what gives them their atavistic character.

The foundational myth provides obscure reassurance as to the unbroken continuity of this filiation, based on a Genesis, and from then on authorizes the community in question to consider this land where it lives, which has now become a territory, as *absolutely* its own.

By an extension of the legitimacy, it happens that, in passing from myth into historical consciousness, the community considers that it has been given the right to extend the limits of this territory. This is what has given 'legitimacy' to all colonizations.

For as long as the earth-totality had not been accomplished, for as long as there were lands to discover, an unknown to conquer, this drive towards the expansion of a territory appeared to be a kind of ontological necessity for the peoples and cultures that believed themselves chosen to discover and govern the world, and who did so.

In the earth-totality that is today physically realized, where creolization has replaced the drive towards expansion and the legitimacy of conquest, the Poetics of Relation enables us to approach the difference between a land (the crucial place of all beings) and a territory (reclamation as the ritual, now infertile, of the Being).

From this point of view modernity is the play, begun anew each time, of this difference and this mutation.

Roche

The time has come when the word becomes its own place. That is to say that it takes itself as its object, not through complacency, nor because it finds itself uprooted from its surroundings, but because it tries to consider whether, out of all the possible places of the world, there is an invariant, a place of places, neither a consensus nor a generalization, but a trace that persists. A trace that would keep alive vigilance, and humour, and the assaults of thought.

Maurice Roche's writing is like this. And it approaches this place of places through suffering, solitude, healthy derision, faced with the stupidity and the derelictions of our human societies. Through laughter, the quietest possible. The writing does not work on the common place in the new sense that we have given to this expression - a meeting of the intuitive thoughts of the world - it brings the common place back down to its sad status as revelation of stupidity. And embroiders the object, explores it, turns it over and over, until we have succumbed to vertigo. I think it is one of the virtues of this writing that it unfailingly inclines us, through the simplicities that it stages and diverts, to this vertigo which leads us into the immeasurability of the world. 'I don't feel well' ['Je ne vais pas bien'] is a common place of the most ordinary kind, and 'I don't feel/go well, but I must go there' ['Je ne vais pas bien, mais il faut que j'y aille'] (the title of one of Roche's novels) is already an introduction to the swaying lilt of a drifting meaning. A writing that dances.

Compact gave us its first music.* To use another of the common places of our time (a fashionable mode or thing), we can say that it is a cult work: one of the rare places, both secret and public, where we see confirmed something inexpressible that we had sensed in the mass of all things. But people say that about so many works whose only effect is to ratify the conventions (the most basic ones) of our collective drives. *Compact* is different: the book resists.

It was written, *literally*, in a multicoloured fashion. A different poet has said, 'life needs all the colours'. We were not aware of this poetic intention, since the first editions of the work were monochrome, classical, even if the diffracted layout and the playful dispersion of the words already alerted

---

* *Compact*, trans. Mark Polizzotti (Illinois: Dalkey Archive Press, 1988).

us to the fact that here was a field of weaves, an unknotting of structures: a different way of practicing writing: 'A texture of signs, of scars, a tactile weave coming apart ...'

The 'object' of the novel is simple and complex (that is to say total): a man is wasting away (dying? waking up?) in his bedroom, or in any other solitary place, a hospital room, an operating theatre, and he goes blind, and he fantasizes, or realizes, the world. 'You will lose sleep as you lose sight.' – 'As you lose sight, you will lose sleep.' To see truly.

The beauty of the new edition of *Compact*, in colours, published by Tristram, means that at first we seem to have been awarded the favour of a more elementary, faster reading – we follow the line of a colour, as they say in planes that we will have to follow a phosphorescent trail to the ground, in the case of an accident – but we immediately realize that this simplicity acted as a mask: the mystery of these words remains, to the extent that they convince us, most importantly, that we are all of us participating 'in everything'.

The clever reader soon finds satisfaction in entering into these colours of the text and specifying them. I tell myself, for example, that all the tones of a novel, from the emotional to the documentary, from the direct address to the confidential, from realism to symbolism, are intervening here. And I believe that I can spot them through an organization that I seem to have guessed: the colours are organized, or rather disorganized, by means of the table of personal pronouns.

The colour green: I.
The black: you singular.
The light orange: he.
The light brown: we.
The white on a black background: you plural.

To which is added the *blue* of any situation described, where the real is captured in the dazzling net of its perception, and the *red*, which corresponds to the impersonal 'one': at the same time I, you singular, he, we and you plural. The 'one' of tragic debate. The 'one' also of the anonymous letter and of clichés. The 'one' of the world bewildered and hunted down.

So. We have understood how it functions. We can read 'linearly', by following one of these colours from one end of the book to the other. There would then be complete series of meanings that would simply marry up, at the point where one colour (a pronoun, a tone, a situation) would take over from another, and be interrupted itself and then come back further on. We hardly stop to ask what symbolism is involved in the choices and attributions of the colours, why the green is for I, why the 'ordinary' printing fonts (in black) are used only for the you singular, which is this I that examines and usually underrates itself? Or is it the demands of the printing works that has decided these attributions? Clever reader, although it doesn't take much (all of that was easy to work out), but conceited as well.

Because he very soon comes across these moments where the green confronts the blue, for example, and the black irrupts into the mass of light brown, like a volcanic island in a sea of faded lava: in other words, these internal articulations of the text as a whole. And it is not linear as we had thought. It requires the pleasure of a different kind of reading. The blue contaminates the green, the light orange pushes the black to its greatest excesses, and we never know how they will all react to being woven together in this way, which both constrains and liberates them. The word works on itself, arises each time from its own birth, its own contradiction, its internal Relation, the enormous duration accumulated from so many revelatory dispersals. The mass that emerges from this is a dizzying Whole-World, which involves us. 'We are the sum of all that'.

It was not so simple and our linear readings (a red reading, a blue reading) were naïve and fallacious. Here, we learn to read by panting hard, by the call of our breaths, by breathing in all the air around us, and I cannot help coming back here to the prose of Michel Leiris, although it is true that this is organized into an obvious weave, whereas Maurice Roche doggedly maintains the gap in the cloth.

They have a great deal in common, despite these opposite rhetorics. The passion for pure geometry, for the plan, for the projection of straight lines between the stars in the sky. The inclination therefore towards an idea or a sensibility of the rough, the exact, the non-lyrical, materials that constitute the solid basis for another distraction, a different kind of vertigo. And then, the word-play, which diffracts the unity of the meaning. Leiris's *Aurora, or aux rats* is echoed in *douleur, doux leurre, d'où l'heure*, which is no less compromising and contaminating. For illness and death, it is never (it is always) the time [*l'heure*].

*

All of History, all the histories, all the languages, all the pidgins, and Old French, the slangs, the digests, the oratory sentence, the musical score, the proverbs, the recipes for just about everything that exists, has been made or imagined, the instructions for use, the graphics, Latin and Greek, Chinese or Japanese characters, and also invisible ink, summaries of texts (which are not the same as digests) or pharmaceutical formulae, all of this organized in a scrum, like in rugby, to be deployed, all of this invading us, readers affected in turn. 'And – regressus ad originem to coincide with the cosmogony – this went backwards through time'.*

*

'One feels more and more cramped as the world grows larger.'** No, really not, dear Maurice Roche, not restricted: fragile, uncertain and threatened, and perhaps a little despairing of so many pitfalls in the world, but as lucid as possible. The proof, *Compact*. This book has brought together for us what was scattered, crossed out (writing like an obstinate scratching), the most beneficial corruptions, and what there will be in his later books of music, of illness and death, an endless dust. But one which comes together as granite, as pillars of lava. As a totem, devastated humanity, carves its shadow in the stone, as a language invents itself within language, like a world. Burst open, winding, its colours shimmering, its subject matter dispersed, and at the same time full and compact. Like a rock [roche]. It seems to me that everything that we shout out in the exaltation and excitement of the world-thought, Maurice Roche carefully invents it, under the accumulation of crossings out, which taken together in(tro)duces – to talk like Roche – such a field of energies. The question remains, for all of us who are perhaps blind to our time: 'How can we now tell apart day and night?' We consult *Compact*, which is our Braille in these shadows.

---

* *Compact*, p. 14.
** *Compact*, p. 10.

'But look, History still goes on rehashing these recalls to the identitarian, based on a territory . . etc.'*

Those are the last desperate bursts of the return of the identitarian repressed. The more the progress of Relation is ascertained, the more creolization grows, the more the madness of those who are panicked by this movement of the world is exacerbated. Their new demon, the absolute Evil that they intend to exorcise, is what they call globalization. Then the places of hybridity and sharing, the Beiruts and the Sarajevos, are systematically crushed and hammered. In the smallest village where a bridge had been built between two communities, this bridge is blown up. The Rwandas are maintained in their dereliction. It would seem that we cannot do anything about it. But we are changing in ourselves, and, all around, there are these breaths of the last night.

---

* *Compact*, p. 87.

The difficulty is that the forces of oppression, which are multinational and whose interest lies in realizing *their* earth-totality, where they will be able to go everywhere to carry out their profiteering, the biggest cities, the smallest island, also make use of a strategy that seems to encourage our relation to the world. 'Open up! Don't close yourself up in your identity'. Which in this case means: 'Give in to the unstoppable necessity of the market'. In this way they hope to dilute you in the current trends. Some peoples resist. Yes, with difficulty. The necessary opposition can in fact sometimes lead to a closing-off and, by a terrible irony, ratify the implicit threat decreed by the capitalist.

❖ ❖ ❖

Objections to this 'Treatise' by Mathieu Beluse, and Reply

Objections
Because this whole environment uproots us. From a single newspaper in a single corner of the world (all countries are corners), in just a single day: The Australian authorities make an official apology to the Aboriginal nations for the widespread abductions of their children perpetrated for decades, children who were submitted to a savage forced assimilation *and then* The murderous fighting in the Congo is increasing (they have forgotten somewhere the refugees from Zaire, one or two million, who knows, or where) *and then* It is not known how many people have been summarily executed in Albania *and then* The waters of the Hague are said to increase leukemia *and then* The Mediterranean is being devoured by seaweed from an improbable source *and then* A man died before crossing the frontier dozens of little packets of cocaine were found in his stomach *and then* A network of child abusers has been dismantled *and then* A man armed with a machine gun enters a school and kills twenty-eight young pupils and their teacher *and then* Holes are appearing in the earth's ozone *and then* The Israeli settlers do not intend to slow down the compulsory occupations of the Palestinian territories *and then* Massacres are spreading all over Algeria *and then* There is an earthquake in Iran, and some just about everywhere in California but they don't count, it's just the usual *and then* The gap between the countries of the North and the South is growing dramatically *and then* The United States is turning the screw on migration, the French are not far behind, there is only Italy where you can enter freely, but perhaps that will not last *and then* The second world summit opens under sombre auspices *and then* The litany of common places, market economy, globalization, multi-ethnic societies, wars and massacres, massacre and war. Imagine what we imagine.

Because, for example, we are only just beginning to realize how barbaric it is to demand that a community of immigrants should 'integrate' into the host community. Creolization is not a fusion, it requires each component to persist, even while it is already changing. Integration is a centralist and autocratic dream. Diversity is at play in the place, runs across different times, breaks and unites voices (languages). A country that creolizes is not a country that becomes uniform. The multi-coloured rhythms of the populations go together with the diversity of the world. The beauty of a country grows from its multiplicity.

Because we sense that the flows of immigration, for which we recognize specific causes (populations fleeing the slaughter of war, people exhausted by famine in their place, the slow sliding of whole collectivities towards the lands of hope) are perhaps also governed by an erratic dynamic, an element of the dream of the world, which mean that we do not understand to what extent or why these flows of immigration begin and then stop. Have the conditions improved in the country of origin? Does the country of destination not provide as many advantages as one might have thought? And what if the flows were more irrational than we thought, and at least of a fractal nature?

Because all of this makes a wave. Across the whole planet, the great waves of music, the heartbreak shared like an elementary - and all the more sacred - communion. But also, the mysterious traces of hybridities that open up all kinds of combined, associated, complicit types of music. Planet-wide, too, the excitements born of watching sporting events, as though the world were a huge Coliseum. Planet-wide the explosions of the common sensibility, which is being perverted with the same obstinacy and as though in a single direction. We don't know what love is, and we don't care. Planet-wide of course is globalization, for which no-one is prepared, although it has been coming for some time. The movements not of workers, as in the good old days, but of workplaces (to where the costs are lowest), which ravage one region without enriching another. The laws of profit, whose undetectable enmeshing obeys a structure of chaos, and which always causes chaos. All the common places of what is vanishing, which are not encounters of the world's thoughts, but a generalized recognition of the same loss full of energies.

Because we guess that what is around us is the true second world, that which expanding techniques are trying elsewhere to create in information technology. We live our life and we live the life of the world. It seems at times that the former is the delusion of the latter, which we cannot control. We live in two or several dimensions, at least when the conditions of our surroundings allow us some space for echoes and, literally, reflection. The novel cannot illustrate this or even become aware of it: the measure of this burning, imperceptible stirring of all the tangled facts of such an Inextricable: not history, but explosions. Or else the novel becomes poetry. Poetry lays the foundation of an imagination that is fragmentary and totalizing, fragile and active.

Because we will have to get used to the increasing lack of differentiation of species, of races, of genres, of viruses or of varieties of the living, (the machine for producing mutants), which is winning without us being able to understand why.

Because we are approaching this new, floating knowledge, which enables you not to go under.

Because we therefore know that we must live inside, or disappear into the distance.

We say that Relation is worldwide and this is not to state the obvious, for we see that not only is its space that of the world, but also that its particular spaces are irrigated by the space of the world. There are certainly closed spaces, from which it is difficult to escape, for all sorts of reasons: economic, political, mental. There are devastated places, whose misfortune maintains their closure. But the space of the world is always present, an invariant. How can we revive this presence in the imagination of a community apparently reduced by its isolation, while at the same time it is fighting against what isolates it?

Reply

Consider the misfortune of peoples. Not only as a moral concern, but because this misfortune, always offended or obliterated, makes up a large part of our knowledge of the world and ourselves.

Consider the work of this knowledge. In our intellectual galaxy, ignorant valuation of the sciences appears possible. We dare to think that we will become involved in this activity of science without losing our way. Because science, via a whole number of techniques, has entered our lives. It is no longer that mythical domain, set apart, impenetrable to common sense, distant and improbable, that it was in the nineteenth century in Europe. It inhabits other places of knowledge, inspired by cultures hitherto despised. There have been so many practical applications of it, which speak to us directly, that we claim quite bluntly to inhabit it. The popularizations seem just as decisive as that which they disseminate. Terrifying genetic manipulations, carried out in secret laboratories, no longer really astonish us. We are capable of discussing them calmly, to disagree with them or accept them. As though the simple fact of talking about them in public constituted a barrier and a protection. Then, because these proliferations of specialisms and their applications have confirmed in the general consciousness the feeling that there is no longer one secret to discover (the 'nub' of the matter) but thousands, and that science now authorizes roundabout routes and unlikely paths. The theories of the sciences of Chaos ('Chaos theory, you know? …') add still more. Erratic systems, invariants, fractal realities are features not only of matter in movement but also of human cultures in interaction. We all feel that that they are adequate for us. Finally, because one whole part of science, perhaps the most adventurous, confirms what we would call an aesthetics: a common background of truth and beauty, without the latter merely being the splendid reflection of the former. There is for us a beauty of the world which is self-sufficient, in truth.

Consider the dissemination of different kinds of knowledge and sensibility. Here is a very particular illustration of these, ironically.

I will sing you a parable, i.e. a very pretentious story.

'The Spirits are the masters that one dreams of. They decide on the Here which is their Centre and the Elsewhere which is allotted to you on the periphery. Ah! You are "the people from over there". All of us, in fact. We insist on arguing that our area is reality and the Centre is a dream. The Spirits are an entity, made up of distinct and imperceptible elements. But these Spirits have created us, we have fashioned them in our minds, and that is how the system works.

'*The Entity of Action*, itself triple (remember, for example, hope faith charity, or liberty equality fraternity, and so on ad infinitum), thinks in a single movement and acts in the same way. Let us stop trying to guess by what mechanisms, but just to know that it works, and the proof of this is our existences brought back, like grey earth in the red earth.

'*The Entity of Permanence* is unique. Its function is not to express or to act but to be. Ah! Being ... Being ... It crumbles parts of time with which it clothes itself and covers "the people from over there". Us, that is.

'*The Entity of Speech* analyses every word from here and from over there (where we have situated ourselves) and throws back into nothingness every utterance that it has judged unacceptable to its taste. We suffer terribly from this. The speaker whose speech is thus diverted into silence finds himself the object of a diminution of presence, let's not say Being, from which he rarely recovers. It is said that this Entity maintains among "the people from over there" - us, that is - courtesans and informers, creating happy and unhappy people. It compares us with each other, which frightens us, it draws up scales and rankings for us. It chooses us.

'The Spirits know that they are the dream of "the people from over there" and that they would vanish if the latter stopped believing in them.'

This is just a parable, a specious story that believes in itself.

The advances or the guesses of the sciences and the plunges or the wanderings of artistic creation are certainly not continuous with each other. It is perhaps this that science and art most definitely share. But the creator ratifies and the scientist supposes: two dimensions of the way of inventing. The artist needs to be convinced that he is right at the moment that he moulds his creation, the scientist needs to doubt, even when he has proved. They both thus invest in the unknown, on the basis of the knowable world. Their relations are of concerted uncertainty, of dreamed certainties. 'That which exists, beyond appearances' – such could be their guarantee of meeting, their best common place.

Measure, Immeasurability

The One magnifies and the Diverse acclaims.

That we are integral to this constellation of humanities. That this does not turn into a system. That the totality is forever totalizing. That the All is not closed nor sufficient. This is living the world.

Dreaming it as well. The magnificence of O. V de L. Milosz!* 'How beautiful is the world, beloved, how beautiful is the world.'

But to dream the world is not to live it. For us, beauty does not grow from the dream, it explodes in the entanglement.

---

* Oscar Vladislas de Lubicz Milosz (1877–1939) was a French poet of Lithuanian origin.

Infinitive of time
Does time ratify legitimacy? Is it not rather
Filiation, desiring and measuring time
Providing duration when duration is lacking
That supports, by nature and right,
Its principle?

When the horde of filiations has tumbled down
Legitimacy vanishes. Then
No more indicator – that arrow – of time
Bursting forth
Projecting, ravaging
In the consuming fire of linearity
The space of the world.

Filiation tried hard to keep the line
Of the generations, it counted out
The almanac of time. But it is
In pain and leprosy, the dry force
That fastened its necessity
Pegged its joint, to the whole
Of this body, all plunder and root
The territory.

Legitimacy was that peg
And this rivet. It was the Shore
From where to set out to conquer, by negating
Happy multi-time, and through the ecstasy
Of root-time.

It is why we have seen
This growing rapacious time-world
Which intended to eat the world
Expel it
Into universal concretion, that is
Into absolute Territory.

And just like the landscapes the countries
Which share and come to life
Are the Finistères of the territory

Open it up into paths, make it infinite
Yes just like that.

To disengage filiation
That absolute of legitimacies, to divert
The supposed time-world from its line,
Is to gush forth in chaos at last
In the multiplicities of time
Which all mean that anyone can envisage it
Or stare it down
Without faltering.

The drifting of languages makes for a painful passion: no-one was more subject to this than Gaston Miron. In a Montreal street, he would stoop down to the pavement, pick up his poor beautiful Quebecker language, and say to me: 'Look, look at these people passing by, they are suffering in their language. Perhaps they cannot pick it up like this. And how could we imagine bilingualism or multilingualism, when they are stealing our language?' I would repeat that for my own part the Creole language was also left abandoned, and many others were disappearing, and that we must go out to meet the languages of the world without confining ourselves to our own voice. He would continue, and of course he was right: 'That's fine, with our guts and our heads, we will hold up high our French languages, and also our Creole languages'. Michael Smith, the murdered poet, worked in a different way, with the singers of Dub poetry, from within the very foundation of the English language. The result was a baroque tension, a raucous concentration of accents, like someone who has already been shouting for too long in a desert. I deplore the fact that I do not know the Arabic language, I cannot appreciate how Mahmoud Darwish takes it into new landscapes, as one can sense from the French translations of his texts. But translation is the very thing that enables us to sense this. Darwish has spoken about the Americas, engaged in his poetry with Columbus, sung the praises of Relation. To open the imagination of languages, to give them new places, is a way of truly combatting uniformities, dominances, standards.

Martinique

Let us say that Utopia is just and enduring when it is shared with everyone. When, shared, it does not descend into presumptuousness and collective madness. Let us forget the politicians' worries, we, the people of Guadeloupe, Martinique and French Guiana. Certainly, we were right not to let those people who in French Guiana had fought against denial, equivocation and injustice languish in prisons built on our land without protesting. In the same way we will be right to join together into a single body to attempt a great work. We are used to thinking in archipelagic terms; let us act, too, in accordance with this fine immeasurability, which is neither disorder nor bewilderment. Let us summon Barbados and Jamaica, Trinidad and Puerto Rico, let us call Cuba and Haiti. See how we graft Utopia onto all these plants of the Creole vegetation. At least, let us propose it. We need them, they need us. No, the notion of need is too limiting. The peoples of the Caribbean are in us, and we are in them. Let's contribute if we can to making these Archipelagos strong places in the world, proudly common places. Let's begin to clean up our surroundings, so that Martinique for example proclaims and maintains itself, integrally, a land of organic products and clarity. Let's stop believing in the production of unsaleable, badly protected commodities, whose fate depends on policies that are always changing and decided elsewhere. Let's no longer limp from readjustments to bankruptcies, from subsidies to job losses. Let's look elsewhere in the world for places where products that we will want, develop, realize through our common determination, could be offered and accepted. In the world there is a place (buyers, people who know what they like and are excited by the exchange) for everything that would come out of a space of light, for everything that would proceed from the determination to clean up the seas and the clouds, the Gardens and the Sands. What is called a market means that the peoples who can do so pay more for the objects and commodities in the world that they know fulfill the assurances that the general mentality is increasingly demanding: untouched by industrial or chemical pollution, conforming to a new kind of beauty in the world and a new health for contemporary human communities. Many others have started along this path. But for us, it is not too late. We believe in the future of small countries, when they form an archipelago like this. Let's remember, as far as we are concerned, that the statutory problems in our relations with France produce nothing but endless badly argued discussions, for as long as independence of thinking, deciding and acting is not there. France is a country that can no longer, apart from its old politicians, afford to coerce another country. It is too fragile within itself, victim of its xenophobic impulses, to sustain another quarrel. If its leaders are not following up on the discussions, it is because we ourselves are not speaking with one voice and perhaps they really do not know whom to believe. The question of the status can be handled from within our position in the Caribbean. Let's speak to France, not to fight against it, nor to be its servants, nor its employees, but to tell it with a single voice that we are going to undertake something different. Let's also explain to France that the norm of its language would soon become obsolete (there are in France shriveled old specialists of this language, just as anachronistic and pretentious as those old politicians we were talking about), if the language did not run the risks of the world. And that we have transmuted it, this language, by taking it with us. As for example the Jamaicans have with the English language or the Cubans with Spanish. Let's seize on this first of all, and first of all from the depths of ourselves: the independence of thought. Let's go openly towards this utopia which we need so much. Let's make Martinique a place of the world, this is our vocation: that is, a place from which we will gradually neutralize the built-up areas that for a long time we believed to be obvious signs of prosperity, where we will regenerate our lands rotten with pesticides, where we will remake the course of our rivers, where we will tirelessly clean up our coastlines so that the fish return, where we will slow down the deadly flood of cars that eat away at the country like ants in an abandoned plate of stew, where we will teach according to our own reference points, thus going to meet up with the forms of knowledge accumulated from all over the world, where we will never again fail to help those young people who go around in nothingness and anxiety, where we will stop having these pointless arguments among ourselves that turn nasty. But let's do it, let's propose it to all, with the calmness of those who do not claim to be teaching others a lesson. Let's stop thinking that our entire crazy consumption of goods, exacerbated by the shenanigans of commerce, can produce happiness. It's not true. Let's not believe that we are the most privileged people of the Caribbean. This over-excited consumption engenders a subterranean uneasiness, which we can nevertheless feel, a hostility between people who do not even know why they can no longer get along. A mediocrity that is unaware of itself. Let's try to make the Caribbean a healthy lung of the Earth, a persistent blue patch in the surrounding grey, until the blue spreads everywhere. Our collective identity is a result of this, but let's not think that it is therefore bastardized. It is the mark and the sign of the unpredictable, to which our imagination is becoming accustomed. Our rhizome-identities are through with essences, exclusivities, the rites of withdrawal. Let's enter our own world, which also means entering the world. Let's make room for all the languages, and our Creole language first of all, because it is an unpredictable resultant, and let's make room for all the *langages*, of the individual or the collectivity, of a poet or a craftsman, which envisage and illustrate the immeasurable diversity of the world. And to this Immeasurability let's apply our Measure, which cannot be a restriction. The measure is the sign of real independence of thought, the gauge of a determination that will not weaken. It is not the narrow dimension of the accepted order or of arbitrary regulations. It does not claim to predict everything in the movement of the world or to make ambitious plans. Our human communities have given up, let's hope, on five-year plans. Measure is boldness and renewal, supported. All peoples are young in the world-totality. There are no more old civilizations that would protect the health of the Whole, like patriarchs draped in ancient wisdom, while other peoples would be burning, almost wild, with a youth not yet tested. Immeasurability has shortened times and multiplied them. To be ancient is to sense most closely the resolution of these times, although it is unpredictable. To be ancient is to flow in unanimity into this movement of the world. Ancientness can no longer be evaluated by a bygone age. We are all young and ancient, on the horizons. Atavistic cultures and composite cultures, former colonizers and colonized, oppressors and oppressed today. We fight the oppressions in our own place, we also open onto the neighbouring islands, and onto all lands. This does not mean leaving our ancestors, either known or unknown. Those who sank to the bottom of the Immense Waters during transportation, those who smothered the fruit of their loins in order to save them from slavery, those who laboured on the Plantations, who marooned in the hills. We must bring them with us as we enter into the renewal of all things. Give a meaning to what they were, which it is so difficult for us to imagine. Look in the face those desperate times that haunt us. Is it necessary to summon up these times? Yes, to open them up. And not to fall back on the old definitions. The advantage of an island is that one can go right round it, but an even more precious advantage is that this trip can never be finished. And see how most of the islands in the world form archipelagos with others. The islands of the Caribbean are among these. Every archipelagic thought is a thought of trembling, of non-presumption, but also of openness and sharing. It does not demand that one starts by defining Federations of States, administrative and institutional orders, it starts everywhere on its work of entangling, without bothering to state the preliminaries. As regards our relations in the Archipelago, let's start with the small things, but while bearing in mind the big ones. We are the higglers* of the Caribbean reality. And let's loudly proclaim this motto: *Martinique, organic country of the world*. It will be a response not to a fashion for ecology, but to precise needs linked to the concerns of ecology. We will adapt as we go along, and it will certainly be a long and difficult process, our organization of work, our distribution of resources, the equilibrium of our societies. It is a hallmark, as long as it corresponds to a reality, which would speak to those who come to our country, to those who would buy its products elsewhere. Yes, difficult and long. We would have to cope with the redeployments of loss, the new habits to create, the stormy periods of adaptation, the need to roll out progressive change, the initial excesses and the individual and collective moments of discouragement. But is our present situation enviable or viable? Can we continue like this? We believe so but immediately we wonder: why this displeasure, this anxiety within us? Isn't the relative comfort of some accompanied by this general malaise, which corrupts us all, and by the absolute lack of comfort of the majority? Will we wait forever for the reassurances and solutions coming from France, and which in this case are not really such? And if we do not dedicate ourselves to this Utopia, will we not anyway have to imagine another one? In what is called the global market, the small countries save themselves by making themselves specialists of very particular productions, that the industrial machine cannot compete with or steal. Let's invent these new products, the fruits of new methods. Let's run this risk. Our responsibility in the matter is collective, and our action should be too. We must make our place immeasurable, that is, link it up with the Immeasurability of the world. Let's also look at its beauty. My hope lies in this voice of the landscapes. The edges of our forests fade into the cultivated lands that lose their momentum in the sands. It is a whole repertoire in miniature. Neither the pineapples nor the bananas really flatten their surroundings. Petite Guinée is next door to Petite Suisse. The Hills are green and red. The great apricot trees provide shade for the Valleys. What is just as beautiful is to find all these landscapes all over the Archipelago, with all the possible nuances and variations. The fabric of our countries raises its volcanoes and plunges into its ravines, sinks under the sea and is reborn, reappears, changed but continuous with itself, in St Lucia or Marie-Galante, Dominica or the Dominican Republic. Let's talk to all those who share such countries with us. And let the Creole Caribbean talk to the world which is itself creolizing. It has brought its

---

* Peddlers.

multiplicity together into a surprisingly convergent diversity. But without any kind of uniformity. Let's consecrate that among us. This is not a Call, nor a manifesto or a political programme. The Call would be, for whoever makes it, the sign of a pre-eminence that has no place here. The manifesto would presuppose putting oneself forward. The political programme would not be suitable or convincing. This is a cry, quite simply a cry. Of a realizable Utopia. If the cry is taken up by some or by all, it becomes speech. A common song. The cry and speech work together to lift up the possibilities, and also what we have always believed to be the impossibilities, of our countries.

One returns to the place, just as one escapes from the story. Mathieu, the one who is not Béluse, glancing accidentally at this text that I am struggling to weave, ingenuously recommends ('wouldn't it be possible, please') that I write as 'he' rather than 'I'. He likes hearing narratives, stories. He authorizes and establishes the art of the novel. I tell him (using 'he') that Mathieu Béluse has come back. He has stopped running through times because, he says, one can no longer move forward. There are people who go to Mars and will soon go to Betelgeuse, but we do not have their techniques. He prefers to spell out the earth, as though he were learning a lesson from it. And if we have to go to Betelgeuse, and soon to Fomalhaut?

Mathieu Béluse consults a branch of shell ginger,* he tries to work out the future. He learns from Marie Celat that impossible art: to inhabit the unpredictable. He enters the archipelago. One does not cultivate this garden, distance is not withdrawal. The Creole garden is stubborn, it takes care of itself and its plants protect each other, like islands banding together. And then, the defeat of time: Oriamé, Désira, Mycéa. The novel remakes itself as marine huts. Mathieu Béluse has come back here.

---

* 'L'à-tous-maux', a plant with medicinal properties.

The narrative used to find its source in the troubled or measured calm of the communitarian, in that requirement that separated it from any other places. Its symbolic system found its meaning there.

Words have moved away from the mysteries of the imperious narrative and from the fragmented fullness of the poem. They have abdicated the narrow confidence of the language. It is as though, given in or fallen from all this clashing around us, they eluded our meanings.

They no longer form planets or galaxies, each one wrapped around its sun or its movement. They disperse themselves into infinity, before this movement explodes and the sun becomes a giant dead star, a burnt dwarf.

In this explosion, which perhaps presages a single primitive and final galaxy – but which one? – narrative loses its symbolic power, those layers of meaning that supported themselves, just as the poem loses that passion for envisaging words as a material, outside the concept.

What does this mean? For someone who sees words as nothing but a familiar neighbourhood, too immediate dreams, the imposition, with no further echo, of the day that passes and the night that goes on forever?

What can this mean, you who advance with no support or gulf in which to place yourself, with no all-powerful heritage or memory, in this sparkling of all new-born things?

Totalities

Creolization is forever envisaging its opposite, and the Archipelago joins with every Switzerland.

A Switzerland? Perhaps, planned by the all-Being, which maintains itself as being-everything.

And what would the Archipelago be? The dispersion of non-Being, which brings together the being of the world.

The being as beings.

Being is immobile in the mountain, it has protected itself from the snow and the impenetrable avalanche.

Non-Being no longer extinguishes the will in the happiness of passivity, nor exacerbates it in blind thrusts. Non-Being does not mean not being.

I was there, not a Being but a painful being, immobile and stiff in this icy downhill street of this village of the Pyrenees, with its few inhabitants. Stuck on these old frozen cobbles, dismayed by my impossible position, shouting to my friends in the distance to leave me alone. Until I decided to jump onto the edge, where streaks of fresh snow at the bottom of the hedge allowed one to hang on and walk. Then I could go down or up, as I wished.

Creolization receives and conceives of the Unique, the unthought of Being, but it also admits the opposite.

The infinite stages of the illusory graduation are all valid, from Being to being, from Switzerland to the Archipelago, in creolization. That amounts to saying that one could not really conceive of a Being-as-being.

The Archipelago is wandering, from land to sea, it is open to the waves and the dawn.

But there are also dawns on the cultivated plain, in the unmoving hills, in the peninsula that watches over the advance of the lands and evokes the unknown. They are inhabited. If they were not, they would deserve to be. These human communities occupy the path, from Being to being.

There are so many identities of peoples, and of a single people when it has undergone changes, that it would be raging madness to try to spell out the norms. To extol every time the absolute contradiction.

Creolization is non-Being finally in action: at last the feeling that the resolution of identities is not at the brink of dawn.* That Relation, that end result of contact and process, changes and exchanges, without losing or distorting you.

We are not told to renounce (being) in order to finally accept (the beings of the world). No, that has not been said, or even supposed. You can escape from that street with the frozen cobbles where you had got stuck, escape to admire at last the surroundings and breathe the cold air.

The multi-energy of creolizations does not create a neutral field where the sufferings of humanity would doze off; it reactivates that dizzying expansion which undoes not differences but the old sufferings born of difference.

This path, from Being to being, to merciful beings! We follow it without disfiguring it.

---

* 'Au bout du petit matin': this is the first line of Césaire's *Cahier d'un retour au pays natal* (Paris: Présence Africaine, 1997).

Yes, our monuments in the Americas! Bois-caïman in Haiti, the Sierra Maestra in Cuba, the Château Dubuc at the end of the Pointe de la Caravelle in Martinique - of which the only remains at ground level are buried traces of the dungeons where the arriving slaves were imprisoned - the ruins of Saint-Pierre, the marks of cleavers on the trunks of the rubber trees that have reappeared around Bélem and Manaus, and so on: what the landscapes, without the help of stone or carved wood, have produced by way of stories and memory, imperceptible but insistent.

But also, in all the spaces roundabout: the Heights of the sky losing themselves in galaxies, the tracts of brush that encumber their own depth, the frantic tastes of the cultivated land, the savannahs with their shadows compressed like bonsaï trees, the sands in the desert that expand your mind, the salt flats where you can study pure geometry, the mangroves inextricably enlaced, the overflowing glaciers, the depths of the sea from where the coming evening rises up, the infinite tundras that overwhelm you, the hills that root you to the spot. Singular and similar, with for each of them not only its word, but its *langage*. Not only its language, but its music.

They say that creolization is an overview, after which we would gain, or profit, from going into specifics. This is to go back to the old divisions, the universal, the particular, etc. They do not know how to read the world. The world does not read itself in them.

Ode to Stone and to Carthage*

see how the *céments* and the *urubes* have united
the village gets together where the ridge is celebrated
the wind distracts yesterday's bean from the fig tree here

this day will come, this day will come

*

from the most fragile wall we have seen, below,
the trireme exhaled into the rust-red sea, and naked
run towards the entry to the Port – the sail swooning on its way

we who are the current and the swell for so many past times

*

is it the rock with the rough brow of the centurion

is it drinking pastis and the misused *serpente*

is it three times the ring that rolls on the breaking wave

listen,

*

urubes, cégaliers, frusques, metals and beautiful doves.
                                                    18 March 1997

---

* The words in italics here are commented on in the section 'Some New Words' (p. 157).

❖ ❖ ❖

The Town,
Refuge for the Voices of the World*

We are beginning to understand that in the margins of the economic and financial wars, which do not primarily benefit nations as such but the multinationals whose circumference is everywhere and their centre nowhere, the real engagements today, the harmonies and disharmonies, the encounters and the conflicts, concern above all the cultures of peoples and communities.

Culture has met up with politics, and the major clashes of our time are marked by this. Politics worked towards the emergence and reinforcement of nations, in Europe and in the expanding West. Culture manifests the anguish and convulsion of intellectual, spiritual or moral entities when placed spectacularly in relation with others, divergent or opposed, in what from now on is for us the world-totality.

This is the moment to remember that the primary intention of the International Parliament of Writers was to meet up to listen to 'the cry of the world'. Multiple contacts between cultures produces this upheaval that re-forms our imaginations, and allows us to understand that we do not abdicate our identities when we open ourselves up to the Other, when we realize our being as a participant in a rhizome – sparkling, fragile and threatened but hardy and obstinate – which is not a totalitarian gathering, where everything would merge into everything else, but a non-systematic system of relation, where we could sense the unpredictability of the world.

---

* Speech given at the Palais de l'Europe in Strasbourg, at the opening of the Congrès du Réseau des Villes Refuges and of the International Parliament of writers (26–28 March 1997).

Imagination. That is to say, art and literature.

It is literature that illustrates this movement of freeing up, which leads from our place to the thought of the world. This is now one of the most important subjects of literary expression. To contribute, using the powers of the imagination, to raising up the network, the rhizome of open identities, who talk and listen to one another.

We can understand why writers, by their very function, become the favourite target of identitarian intolerance.

Exchange, the shared total of teachings and information on everything that stirs up and fertilizes the thought of the world. The intellectual, the journalist, the artist are by the same token, by their very function, the prioritized goal of all the forces of imprisonment and exclusion.

And when they find themselves, the intellectual, the journalist, the artist and the writer, isolated in a place of the world, it is not only their voice that is gagged, but their life that is destroyed. The right to existence and the right to expression are tragically merged in the same denial.

Relation, that is also a Poetics, in the active sense of the word, which raises us up in ourselves, and solidarity, whereby we manifest that raising up. Every network of solidarity is in this sense a true Poetics of Relation.

It may seem contradictory to use this term, a Poetics, of an enterprise, the network of Refuge Towns, that has required and still needs so many administrative arrangements and institutional decisions, and calls on us to surmount so many barriers put up by custom, the rule of the ordinary or simply habit. But I will take this risk.

For this is not only a question of a humanitarian action, although that could have sufficed. The Refuge Town is not like a charity home, it is involved with the guest it has chosen to welcome in relations of mutual knowledge, of gradual discovery, of long-term exchange, which make this enterprise a truly militant exercise, an active participation in the general meeting 'of giving and receiving'.

As with everything concerning the intentions or actions of the International Writers' Parliament, and also in accordance with the explicit wishes of the Towns that have undertaken the setting up of this network, none of the actions that result from it are linked to a partisan politics. It is when it frees itself from political bias and its limitations that cultural action most truly encounters the political dimension, which illuminates for us both the country in which we live and the world that calls out to us.

The Town, Refuge for the Voices of the World

Imagination, exchange, Relation.

A town, which can be the place of so much suffering, injustice, stifled unhappiness, despair without horizons, then becomes, entering into the world's imagination and completing this exchange and enacting Relation, the symbol and the vector of new hopes.

A town, a modern town, is a piece of land, a root identity, but not unique and not a single root, it is also a relational identity.

A town brings together and symbolizes the region in which it is based, but it is equally open to the systems of relations that have been woven between the cultures of the world.

The town is regional within the nation, it is national within the system of the world, but it returns to its particularity when it is a question of accepting the particularity of the Other.

It 'understands', that is it ratifies, the set of values from which it has come. It 'understands', that is it authorizes and illustrates, the relation between the values that have come from everywhere, that it welcomes and protects.

In this way the modern town can be the refuge of the voices of the world.

It is to the credit of the towns of Europe that they have responded so wholeheartedly to the call from the International Parliament of Writers and have set up this rhizome of solidarity and freedom of expression.

Perhaps they have been inspired or helped by traditions of struggle for their emergence, fighting for their freedom, determination to improve living standards, traditions that go back a long way in their history.

It is my wish that they will also work together to extend this network to other continents, to other urban communities that have fewer resources. The rhizome must spread and multiply further afield.

Let us listen to the cry of the world.

Let us go beyond the petty obligations of the everyday, and follow the procession of these writers and artists who have travelled far from their homes; let us agree that they have contributed a great deal, helping us to weave this network.

From everywhere, the mass graves and the genocides, the camps of ethnic purification, the wars that can never be expiated and the generalized massacres, the appeal rises up from human communities demanding to be recognized in their specificity, but also, sometimes expressed by these same oppressed and suffering communities, as in the Mexican Chiapas, the idea that every specificity would suffer from being closed off and self-sufficient.

To speak of one's surroundings, one's country: to speak of the Other, of the world.

We now know that any culture that isolates and closes itself gradually falls into malaise and discomfort, into this imbalance that is all the more upsetting in that one can see no plausible reason for it. The individual there is like an overheated oven, that nothing can turn off.

Then the most terrifying thing, far worse than the yelling and hatred face to face, is the everyday 'normality', calm and innocent, closed in on itself, of the statements of exclusion and rejection of the other.

Against this background drone of horror, those who have the vocation to speak out preserve the vivacity of the word, which they send all over the world. It is once again to the credit of those in charge of public life to help them to do so.

Freedom of existence, freedom of speech, freedom of creation.

The Town, Refuge for the Voices of the World

Some New Words

They have formed in the fullness of writing, not in its hollows and gaps, and it is noticeable that they are all in the plural. This is because, apart from *serpente* which has its antecedent, they perhaps fear the singularity of Being. They come together and multiply each in itself, knowing that they are ephemeral. The beauty of the word that will soon perish. Would it not have been better to leave them in the wandering of the poem where they appeared, without now explaining them? To define them would already be to kill them. The definition will turn around them.

Xamaniers – trees that produce xamanas. Trees of trees, therefore.

Arapes – ploughs for working tarmac.

Daciers – warders and magistrates with steel daggers, literally.

Salènes – campion and *salines* (salt flats): living and unlikely plains.

Huques – cube-shaped buildings, forming huts. Ruins, in the cold and luxurious light of the windows.

Céments – not cement, but its magnet, which attaches in all different ways, instead of dividing.

Urubes – the pastoral charm in Ur, the wheat-bird.

Serpente – an endless grass.

Cégaliers – in Mediterranean countries, regular clumps of cicadas, forming sonorous roots.

Frusques – the old clothes of time, which make their wearer brusque. Not to be confused with *frusques*, which has given us *saint-frusquin* (belongings).

Indications of Most of the Places and Occasions

The Carrefour des Littératures européennes, the International Writers' Parliament, The Centre of French and Francophone Studies at Baton Rouge, Rutgers University, the Musée des Arts d'Afrique et d'Océanie, the Institut du Monde arabe, Tokyo University, Perpignan University, the Prix Carbet de la Caraïbe, the Université des Antilles-Guyane, the Bibliothèque François-Mitterand, The City University of New Yor (CUNY), the Parliament of Navarre, the University of Almeira, the Assises de la Traduction in Arles, Columbia University, the Basque country, New York University (NYU), the Boréales of Normandy, the Town Hall in Lamentin.

And also the following publications: *Littératures, Le Nouvel Observateur, Yale French Studies, L'Esprit créateur, Dédale, Croissance, L'Oriflamme, Le journal du dimanche, Les Inrockuptibles, Al Cantara, Édouard Glissant, poesia y politica*, by Diva Barbara Damato, *La letteratura caraïbica francofona*, by Carla Fratta, *Littératures antillaises d'aujourd'hui*, edited by Cathie Delpech.

Let us also name, for the pleasure of exchange: Carminella Biondi and Elena Pessini at Parma, Alexandre Leupin at Baton Rouge, Bernadette Cailler in Florida, Jean-Pol Madou in Miami, Geneviève Bellugue in Paris, Adonis the lyrical in Beirut, Michael Dash in Jamaica, Nancy Morejon in Cuba, Celia Britton in Aberdeen, Édouard Maunick in Durban, Gérard Delver in Guadeloupe, Henri Pied at *Antilla*, Jérôme Glissant on the old road leading to *Pays-mêlés*, Jayne Cortez and Melvin Edwards in New York, Thor Vilhjálmsson in Iceland, Emilio Tadini in Milan, Piva and her Vernazza dialect, Christian Salmon in all our meetings, Jacques Coursil in Fort-de-France, Patrick Chamoiseau at La Favorite, Alain Baudot in Toronto.

The poem *Hommage à Pierre et à Carthage* has appeared in a single manuscript edition accompanied by pastels by Sylvie Sémavoine.

www.ingramcontent.com/pod-product-compliance
Lightning Source LLC
Chambersburg PA
CBHW071411300426
44114CB00016B/2266